BRIGHT IDEAS

History Projects

CW01426394

Written by Florence Beetlestone

Published by Scholastic Publications Ltd,
Villiers House, Clarendon Avenue,
Leamington Spa, Warwickshire CV32 5PR

© 1993 Scholastic Publications Ltd

Written by Florence Beetlestone
Edited by Juliet Gladston
Sub-edited by Jane Wright
Illustrated by Nick Ward
Designed by Sue Limb
Front and back covers designed by
Keith Martin
Photograph by Martyn Chillmaid
Artwork by Steve Williams Design,
Leicester.
Typeset by Typesetters (Birmingham) Ltd
Printed in Great Britain by Clays Ltd

**British Library Cataloguing in Publication
Data**
A catalogue record for this book is available from the
British Library.

ISBN 0-590-53087-9

Contents

Introduction

OUTLINE OF THE BOOK

History Projects has been divided into two main sections. The first section uses the National Curriculum supplementary study units (SSUs) as the basis of themes, and the second looks at the history that is to be found in non-history themes. 'A past non-European Society' has been omitted from the first section as this area is so vast that it could form a book on its own. Both sections are divided into seven themes. The activities in each theme are supported by a topic web. The topic webs in the first section have been designed so that you can see how the SSU theme can support work in all subject areas and therefore provide an excellent framework for a whole term's work. The topic webs in the second section show a range of history topics that can be followed when working on non-history themes such as 'Pattern'.

You will notice that many of the ideas in the webs and in the activities over-lap. This should help you to use many of the themes in an interrelated way. For example, ideas appearing in 'Pattern' can easily be followed under 'Houses and places of worship' where you might look at patterns in religious artefacts, or wallpaper design. Similarly when looking at 'Food and farming' you could use ideas from the 'Materials' section, researching the materials used to make farming tools and equipment. The SSU themes can be followed in all the non-history themes in this book and in most themes which you might wish to follow.

WAYS OF WORKING

The activities can easily be extended to take up several sessions. Historical concepts are best grasped by a gradual process of development and understanding. These activities will be more effective if developed over several sessions or repeated with different aspects, materials, varying methods and so on. They are not 'one-offs' but provide a means of exploring the historical aspect of themes. This means that the activities will need to be supported by research, which will take several sessions. The activity will provide the necessary starting point.

The activities which follow have all been given an approximate appropriate age range covering both Key Stage 1 and Key Stage 2. However, all can be adapted to suit any age or to meet particular requirements.

THE PHOTOCOPIABLE SHEETS

The photocopiable pages at the end of the book are intended either to provide some additional reference material, such as the canal map, or to provide activity sheets, such as the stamp blanks. The intention is to provide a variety of supporting sheets so that your own ideas are sparked off, and the sheets used to develop your own ideas.

HISTORICAL APPROACH

The activities in this book are intended to support the National Curriculum and foster the skills, knowledge and concepts required. History needs to be taught in a variety of ways.
● The examination of historical artefacts: these may be in situ, brought into the classroom or form part of a museum exhibit. The children will learn most from handling rather than just looking at the artefacts, so it is important to build up your own class collection.
● Looking at pictures, portraits and photographs: these provide a vital and often detailed window on the past. You will need to help children to read the information, since it can be interpreted in various ways.
● Drama and role play: re-enacting past events helps to develop chronological awareness. It also enables children to empathise with past characters and understand some of the decisions these characters had to make. Role playing can further develop these skills allowing children to exercise their judgements and to interpret events. They need to realise how history is often not interpreted in the same way.
● Stories: these help children to relate immediately to the people and events from the past. The lives of past people are always fascinating, particularly when children look at experiences similar to their own – parents, schooldays, pets, toys and so on. Historical events are often full of excitement and drama. Try retelling events in your own words if the details seem dry or remote.
● Discussion: children need to consider what they are trying to find out, what they already know and how they will set about finding information. They need to discuss ideas, interpret evidence and debate conclusions. In this way they will be able to appreciate other viewpoints and interpretations.

• Use of primary source material: all decisions about the past should be based on evidence, e.g., 'How do we know that the school was built in 1898?' We can find the evidence in the foundation stone and the school's log book. The children will need to consult a variety of records, diaries, note-books, drawings, census material and so on. There is also a mass of information available in libraries, museums and archives. You will need to train your children how to find this material and how to use it.

• Visits: much historical evidence is to be found in the environment, whether it be local housing, a church, a factory, a bridge or castle. The children will need to be taken out on class visits quite regularly to draw upon this evidence. Further information will arise from visits to galleries, museums and heritage centres.

• Activities: enabling the children to make similar artefacts to ones from the past and try out similar processes such as making and using a quill pen helps them to understand some of the processes involved in the past and to appreciate some of the contexts. It also helps to create an empathy with the past which forms the basis of all historical investigation.

MONITORING AND RECORDING CHILDREN'S WORK

Discussion and written work will provide you with some evidence of how well the children are meeting the attainment targets. If you use photocopiable page 101, this will help children to identify their own learning and provide you with an analysis which you can use for your own records and reports. The sheet is divided into three columns: 'K' indicates what the children already know; 'W' what they would like to know, and 'L' is to be filled in at the end of the topic to show what the children have learned. Go through these categories with the whole class, so that they all understand what to do with their own sheets.

When groups are set research tasks they should fill in a group sheet. Individuals can complete their own sheets when working on their own. Encourage everyone to complete the 'L' column at the end of the topic. You will find this information extremely valuable for record-keeping!

BUILDING UP A CLASS/SCHOOL RESOURCE BANK

Tacking a history syllabus successfully means having a range of materials and artefacts available to use. Build up a stock of old postcards and photographs, old magazines, old children's books, toys, household goods, memorabilia and collectibles about transport, local history, clothes and so on. All of these items can be obtained quite cheaply at jumble sales, car boot sales and antique fairs. Collect postcards from museums and galleries and try to collect a range of local maps and records such as the census for a few local roads in, say, 1841, 1871 and 1891. In particular your school should try to build up a good collection of records and artefacts about the school's history.

THE SCHOOL IN HISTORY

Using history SSUs as the basis of themes

Ships and seafaring

Vocabulary chart

Age range
All ages.

Group size
The whole class.

What you need
A large detailed picture of a ship, a large felt-tipped pen, flip chart, photocopiable page 102.

What to do
Lead off the class discussion about the ship in your picture. Talk about such things as its means of propulsion – e.g. wind, sails, oars, steam; consider some of the features; look at the design; discuss what life on board would be like and so on. Ask the class to name as many features of the ship as they can. List the words on the flip chart. Infants should be able to provide most of the basic words, while junior children should be encouraged to research the more detailed vocabulary needed, for example, the types of sail, the names of knots and so on.

Give each child a copy of photocopiable page 102 and ask them to fill in as many words as possible from the flip chart on to the correct area of the ship on the photocopiable. Older children may like to fill in their own words.

Follow-up

Using their vocabulary charts the children can work in pairs and groups to write about what life would have been like on board the ship in the picture. Encourage the children to extend their knowledge by looking at different aspects such as food arrangements and navigation, researching appropriate information. The class stories can be put together to make a class book.

Model boats

Age range
Five to six.

Group size
Individuals or pairs.

What you need
Balsa wood, Plasticine, paper, a piece of bark, scissors, a knife (not too sharp), adhesive, sticky tape.

What to do
Tell the children that they are going to construct small hollowed-out boats from different materials, and test their ability to float. Encourage the children to create a coracle shape with Plasticine, so that it is almost like a floating bowl. They should then hollow out the centre of the balsa wood *carefully* with a knife to create a similar shape. The piece of bark can be shaped similarly by rounding it and gluing if necessary. Finally, they should create a paper boat by making a box design and sticking it together with sticky tape.

Having made their boats the children should test them to make sure that they all float. Which one do the

children think will be most effective? Put LEGO or Playmobile people inside. Which one do they think will sink first? Ask the children to record their predictions onto a chart like the one illustrated above.

They should then float their boats in the water and see which one sinks first. Why do they think this happened? Which material makes the strongest boat and why?

Follow-up
Which of the materials that the children used – paper, Plasticine, bark and balsa – do they think would have been available in the past? Which materials do they think could be best adapted to make a full-size boat?

Ask the children to find pictures of coracles. If you can obtain small pieces of leather they can try to make a coracle by gluing the leather to a frame made from light spills which bend into shape. Why might skins be a popular choice as a boat building material?

Ship rummy

Age range
Five to seven.

Group size
Two groups – one of six and one of seven.

What you need
Reference books showing a variety of ship designs from different periods; playing-card sized pieces of drawing paper; thin card, coloured felt-tipped pens, laminator or clear self-adhesive plastic.

What to do
Ask each child to choose a particular type of ship from the reference books. Try to ensure that there is a balance of type. Each child should then copy their ships very carefully on to playing-card sized paper putting as much detail as possible into their drawings. They should write the approximate date and type of vessel underneath each drawing. Photocopy each drawing four times on to thin card. The children now need to colour their four cards in exactly the same colours, so that the four cards are identical. (If you have a colour photocopier then they need only colour one design and copy it four times). Laminate the cards or cover them with clear self-adhesive plastic.

The children will now have fifty-two cards which can be used to play a rummy-type game. The object of the game is to get two sets of ships (one of three cards and one of four cards) before your partner.

The rest of the class could work on a similar game, using different designs or other aspects of the topic. The cards could be used in a simple matching activity or used to create a time-line or used in pairs for a memory game. Alternatively these or similar cards can form the basis of lotto games.

A very simple logic game could also be made by devising stylised cards which depict boats with, for example, a given number of sails, masts or oars and/or are coloured in different colour combinations. The children could then use them to make sets of, for example, 'all the green Viking longboats' or 'all the red clippers'.

Follow-up
Instead of drawing the ship design on to paper, children could draw directly on to pressprint polystyrene in order to make printing blocks. They could then print four identical cards. These printing blocks could be used to make a ship time-line, printing the ship types in chronological order on to a sea frieze. They could also be used to decorate artwork and wall displays, for example, as a border around a display of writing about seafarers.

Trade route board game

Age range
Seven to nine.

Group size
Small groups of four to six.

What you need
Reference books showing routes covered by explorers and traders such as Sir Walter Raleigh, Sir Francis Drake and Henry Hudson, or maps showing the routes covered by specific commodities such as silk or salt; a large map of the world or particular continents covered by the chosen routes; strong piece of card of fit the size of the map; coloured pens, small pieces of card for game cards, counters, dice, paper for illustration, glue.

What to do
Tell the children that they are going to design a board game based on a trade such as the silk road. They should copy the appropriate continents or countries in pencil on to a piece of card. Next they should mark out the route which will form the route of the game. They should design appropriate rewards and pitfalls to make the game exciting. They should use clues that are appropriate to the route, for example, 'Camel train set upon by Persian raiders – go back three spaces'. Where possible some dates should be used, so that the game is set in a particular period. They can make counters, game cards and/or dice as needed.

When the design has been completed the board and any cards should be coloured and laminated or covered in clear self-adhesive plastic.

Different groups can work on different routes. Stick to a class theme – either explorers or commodities. Try to research as much background information as possible.

Follow-up
The class will now have about half a dozen games which will reinforce the idea of trade. They can date the routes and put the games in chronological order and make a large wall map of the world and indicate the various routes on it. How many overlap? Are any patterns of exploration and development emerging? Why was the cost of silk, for example, so high? Who would have worn silk?

The children should produce short written pieces giving further information about the routes, towns, people and commodities involved to accompany their maps.

Viking longboat

Age range
Eight to ten.

Group size
Individuals, pairs or small groups.

What you need
Date box or box of similar shape and size, cardboard, scissors, small pieces of dowelling, used matchsticks, small pieces of fabric, twine, paints, glue, Plasticine.

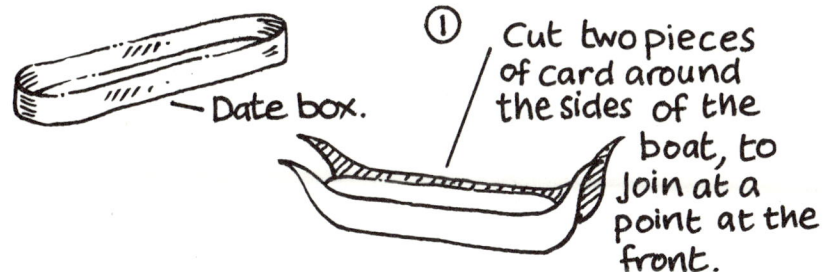

Date box.

① Cut two pieces of card around the sides of the boat, to join at a point at the front.

② Draw two figureheads then glue to the point at the front of the boat.

Twine to anchor mast

Dowelling for mast.

③

Plasticine

④ Design and colour a card sail with a distinctive figurehead

Oars (matchsticks)

Viking shields. (Card discs)

What to do
Ask the children to make models of Viking longboats. They should use a date box as the hull of the boat and measure pieces of card to cover the sides to make a longboat shape. The ends should curve upwards and they should make them long enough so that they can be glued together in a point. The children can then design a figure-head for the front of their boats. Tell them to cut out two figure-head shapes from card and glue these together over the front of the boat. They can construct a sail using dowel for the masts and anchor it to the boat with twine. They should fix the mast in the centre of the date box with a small piece of Plasticine.

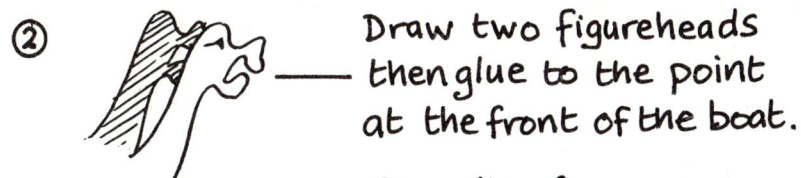

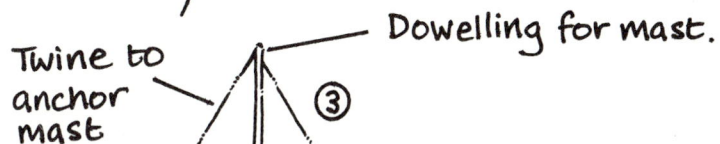

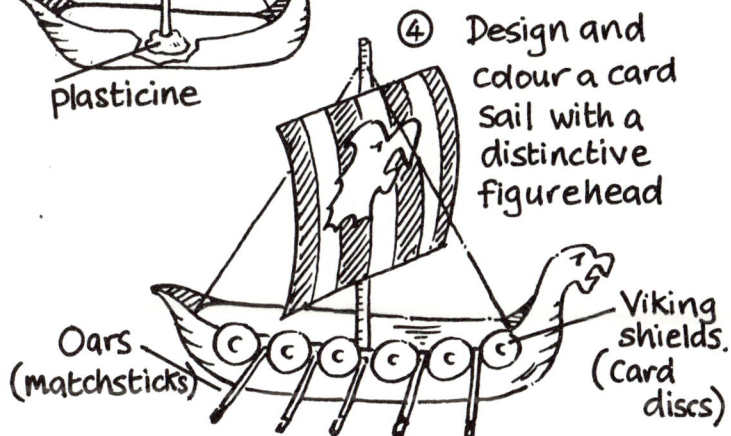

Finally, let the children paint their boats and make round card shields to line the sides. They can also use matchsticks to make oars and Plasticine to make miniature viking oarsmen. Each Viking should be given a shield and oar and fixed into place into the boat.

Several pairs of children can make boats, making them distinctive with different sail cloth patterns and figureheads. Some of the class could research typical figurehead designs. What was their purpose? Why was the shape of the longboat so effective for both inland and sea travel?

Follow-up

The boats can be displayed in a three-dimensional landscape representing either a harbour, fiord or battle scene. Papier mâché can be used to create the scenery on a baseboard (strong cardboard or hardboard is ideal). The children should research the appropriate scenery and clearly indicate where they are setting their scene. Perhaps they could reconstruct a Viking scene from their local area in that period. (Local archives should be able to help here.) A harbour scene could include domestic buildings, shops and models of crafts people.

Armada computer game design

Age range
Nine to eleven.

Group size
The whole class and small groups.

What you need
Reference books about the Armada, paper, pencils, felt-tipped pens, examples of computer adventure games, computer magazines with examples of layouts of computer adventure games.

What to do
Most children will be familiar with the typical layout of computer adventure games – the idea of moving around from 'room' to 'room' at different levels with each 'room' representing a different scene in the game. The children will also need to be familiar with the story of the Armada. They should be able to retell it listing key events and features.

Work with the whole class picking out six or seven events from the story of the Armada in chronological order, for example, Queen Elizabeth addressing the troops at Tilbury, the Spanish ships running aground at Tobermory Bay and so on. Decide which events might be suitable scenes to develop in a game form.

Each group of children should then work on a particular scene. They will need to design the layout and indicate how the characters will move through that scene to the next. Hazards and rewards should be built in. Make sure that each scene fits together to make chronological and effective progression through the Armada story. You might also like to consider whether you wish to have different levels of ability in the game.

If you have access to a game design programme the Armada game could actually be developed on the computer. However, as this is unlikely, the children should concentrate on making the design of the game as straightforward as possible. If the designs and instructions are put together clearly they could be sent to a computer software company who might be interested in producing it commercially.

Follow-up
The children can write their own accounts of the Armada imagining that they are the characters in the game. These can be illustrated in cartoon form, and made into individual books and a wall story.

The story of Nelson

Age range
Nine to eleven.

Group size
The whole class and small groups.

What you need
Reference books on the life of Lord Nelson, paper, card, fabric scraps, junk materials.

What to do
Read several versions of the life of Nelson to the class. You should then work together to decide upon six key events in his life. Divide the class into six groups and give each group one of these events. Each group should then write a script which covers this event, so that each scene can be put together to form a play about Nelson's life.

When each group has written their script they should design appropriate costumes and props to suggest the period. If possible visit a museum or gallery to look at costumes or paintings of that time.

The finished play can form the basis of an assembly.

Follow-up
Ask the children to try and find out why Nelson was considered such a hero. Would he be considered a hero today? What happened to the men he defeated? How might he have felt? The children can write accounts imagining that they were sailors on board Nelson's flagship or were on board one of the defeated French ships. Can they find out anything about their local area during the Napoleonic Wars? Many local archives contain records of local volunteer militia, for example, or special defences may have been built locally.

Use a similar approach to research other historical characters. Again try to decide why particular people were, and have remained famous.

Links with other curriculum areas

Art – boats in art
- making models;
- painting;
- drawing;
- famous paintings.

History
- ships through the ages;
- trade ships;
- explorers;
- invasion and settlement;
- war and naval battles;
- museums: visit to a ship, e.g., Cutty Sark.

Technology
- movement of different types of objects;
- boat construction;
- rowing, wind-sail, steam.

English – sailors:
- in stories and poems;
- lives of famous sailors;
- their diaries and accounts;
- press gangs.

Ships and seafarers

Science – boats
- materials used?
- where?
- how?

Geography
- area census;
- ports, markets, etc.;
- how local areas were/are affected;
- journeys of explorers;
- trade routes;
- navigation.

RE
- customs/rituals – burials and marriages at sea.

Maths
- data collection:
  - size of ships
  - measurements
- area of hold capacity.

PE
- movement of the sea
- dramatic movement representing storms, shipwrecks, etc.

Food and farming

Farm/food display table

Age range
All ages.

Group size
The whole class.

What you need
A display table, backing cloth, books and pictures illustrating old tools and implements, a collection of artefacts which represent some aspect of food production. (You may need to vary this according to where your school is located. If you are in a rural area it should be possible to have access to old farming tools and implements. In urban areas, if it is not possible to borrow items from local museums, it should be possible to find examples of old garden tools or kitchen/cooking equipment.)

What to do
Tell the children that they are going to create a farming/food display which represents, as far as it is possible, their local area and backgrounds. Together look at a series of reference books which show old tools and implements. Then, ask the children to bring in any old tools which they may have at home which relate to food production, giving examples of such things as old Dutch hoes, trowels and kitchen gadgets which they might be likely to have.

Visit jumble sales and antique fairs yourself and collect a few small items. It is fairly easy to pick up things like cheese graters, mincers and butter pats very cheaply. If possible, take a group of children to a junk shop to look for other examples. It may also be possible to borrow groups of things from local museums.

Set up the items on the table and where possible, give some idea of the date of each object. Try to get similar new items so that the collection can be categorised into old/new if dating is difficult.

Use the items to encourage close observation skills. The children can make detailed drawings of the objects and display them alongside the objects. Discuss what the objects are made from and how they were likely to have been made and used. Ask the children to write a short piece about each item. If you have several similar items, jelly moulds for example, the children can try to arrange them in chronological order.

Symbols of harvest

Age range
Six to eight.

Group size
Small groups.

What you need
To make the dough: 1,000g plain flour, 200g salt, ½ litre water; rolling pins, knives or cutters, baking tray, clear varnish, small polythene sandwich bags, paints (if needed), access to an oven.

What to do
Explain to the children that before industrialisation, rural life was dependent on the farming year. The importance of key farming events such as sowing the seed, ploughing and harvest was marked by customs and religious festivals. At harvest time tokens, dollies and symbols were made in order to ensure a good harvest.

The children can use modelling dough to make various harvest symbols. To make the dough they should mix all the ingredients together and then knead it repeatedly until as much air as possible has been removed from the dough (at least ten minutes). As this recipe uses salt as a preservative it will dry out fairly quickly, so the children should keep it in a polythene bag until they are ready to use it. When they are ready to work with it the children should take out small pieces of dough at a time and model each piece before using the next piece. They should model something connected with harvest such as apples, grapes, a bowl or fruit, a sun, fish, a harvest loaf and so on. They may like to copy a design or design their own models. If the children want to make hanging decorations they should make a hole in the model somewhere near to the top.

Once the models are complete, put them on a baking tray and place them in the oven for 30 minutes at gas mark 1–2 or 100°C. When the models have cooled completely they can be painted and varnished and hanging models can be threaded with a small piece of ribbon.

Follow-up
Ask the children to make a collection of different types of bread and preserve them by baking them in a low oven for around 30 minutes and then varnishing them. They could also collect pictures of different types of bread and find out about harvest loaves and how bread is used in harvest customs. Grow grains of wheat and read to the children the story of the 'Little Red Hen'. Use this to introduce a topic on bread production through the ages. Discuss why bread has always been a staple diet. Look at changing techniques for flour production.

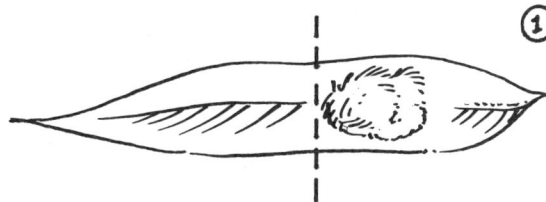

① Fold a maize leaf with a piece of cotton-wool inside and tie it securely.

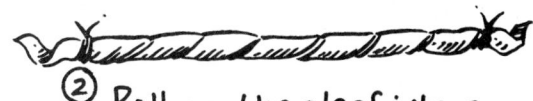

② Roll another leaf into a long tube and tie off each end to make hands.

③

b.) Make a slit here for head.

a.) Cut the ends off a large leaf and fold over in half to make body. Tie at waist.

④ Place head through slit and insert the arms.

Maize dollies

Age range
Six to eight.

Group size
Small groups.

What you need
Fresh maize leaves (about three per child), light-coloured cotton, cotton wool, scissors.

What to do
Tell the children that maize dollies were made from one crop in order to ensure that the next harvest was a good one. Corn dollies were similarly made from the straw after the corn was cut.

Using the diagrams as a reference, give each child half a maize leaf and tell them to put a piece of cotton wool in the centre of the leaf. They should then fold the leaf around the cotton wool and tie it with cotton to form the head of a doll. Give each child another leaf and tell them to roll it into a long tube and tie off the ends to form hands. The children can use a large leaf to make the main body. They should cut the narrow ends off it and fold it in half. Tell them to cut a slit in the fold and fit the head piece through. Finally, they can slide the arms in and tie a piece of cotton round the waist to form the doll.

Follow-up
Collect reference books which show examples of maize and corn dollies. Craft books are often a good resource. Ask the children to find out from these books why such dollies were used. What are the customs associated with them? Are there differences in national and regional customs? For example, are particular corn dolly designs associated with particular areas? Ask the children to write about these customs and perhaps copy some of the ways of weaving and plaiting straw (either using real or craft straws). If the children have any examples of this at home (they are often sold as souvenirs) they could bring them in for display.

Farming year frieze

Age range
Eight to ten.

Group size
The whole class and small groups.

What you need
A collection of postcards and illustrations from museums and galleries showing life on the land before the twentieth century; sets of pictures such as the Duc de Bury's *Book of Hours* (in the British Museum) provide an excellent example of medieval life over the seasons; art materials.

What to do
Discuss as a class some of the significant events in the farming year. The ritual of sowing, reaping and ploughing has changed little over the centuries, and in England has been commemorated by a number of local and regional customs, for example, Plough Monday and Harvest Festival. After consulting reference books and picture postcards decide together upon a set of four seasonal scenes depicting the farming year before the Industrial Revolution. You should decide on a particular period and then the children can work in groups to research the relevant information for haymaking, ploughing, milking and so on.

Once they have gathered enough resource material they can begin to translate this information into pictorial form. The children should then choose whichever medium they prefer – paint, collage and so on – and work to create a wall frieze of farming customs, methods and rituals of the chosen period.

Follow-up
Ask the children to choose one of the postcards, such as Constable's *The Hay Wain* or a cornfield painting by Van Gogh and use it as a basis for close observational art work. They should then copy the picture as accurately as possible. Groups of children might like to look at how particular artists have represented the pastoral scene and then write about the techniques they used. They could think about texture, colour and form shape and look at who is in the picture, what they are doing and the methods that are being used. Is our idea of rural life in the past coloured by such images? How realistic are they? Do they really represent the toil and hardship of rural life?

Read to the children extracts from novels such as Thomas Hardy's *Tess of the Durbervilles* which give accounts of rural hardship. Try to find contemporary accounts of past rural life in your area and let the children compare these with some of the images shown in many paintings.

Make a collection of poems and songs about farming and rural life. As a class you could use John Clare's *The Shepherd's Calendar* as the basis for a similar frieze. This could be divided into monthly sections. Alternatively, the class could produce a 12 section zigzag book, combining writing and illustration, to complement the poem.

Animal histories

Age range
Eight to eleven.

Group size
Small groups.

What you need
Reference books about farm animals; art and craft materials, postcards and photographs of old breeds.

What to do
Ask each group to choose a particular farm animal – cow, horse, pig, sheep, chicken and so on. They should then research into the different types of that animal that are bred today and look at some of the varieties.

Some of these old breeds have been preserved in farm museums. If possible arrange a visit to one. If this is not possible, then try to obtain leaflets and postcards from various museums instead. There are often farming groups and organisations which specialise in the sale of rare breeds and these too should provide a useful source of information. Consult your yellow pages and local libraries.

Once each group has gathered as much information as they can they should draw examples of old and modern breeds and represent them in sets according to age of breed. Small papier mâché models of the animals can also be made and displayed in models of old/new types of fields.

How have the breeds changed? Why did such a change take place?

Follow-up
Ask the children to look for references to animals in books, paintings and so on. Ask them to date these examples as far as possible, and arrange them in date order.

Try to locate old farming memorabilia examples in your local archives which might refer to cattle sales, market prices, foot and mouth disease outbreaks and so on. Obtain photocopies of these and let the children use them to make group books about each animal type. They can make each book in the shape of the animal the book is about.

Ask the children to research local customs such as the right of commoners to graze their cattle on common land. Do such rights still exist?

Medieval field system

Age range
Nine to eleven.

Group size
The whole class and individuals.

What you need
Ordnance Survey maps of the locality, colouring pens or pencils, paints, card, papier mâché, reference books and pictures, photocopiable page 103.

What to do
Discuss as a class how the manorial system worked. Using photocopiable page 103, study of the layout a typical feudal village – with manor, manor farm, church, houses for yeomen, villeins, serfs and so on. Discuss with the children how society was graded and how life was regulated by the lord of the manor.

Consider the way farming was organised and the three-field system (a rotating system of two fields cultivated for crops, while one lay fallow). Ask the children to look at current Ordnance Survey maps and see if they can find examples of this field system which still exist today. Can they see any evidence on the map of this early manorial framework? (Boundaries are often indicative of old manorial lands and churches and manor houses often still stand side by side). Ask the children to write about their findings. Encourage each child to colour in their sheet.

Work with the children to make a three-dimensional model of a manorial village clearly showing the field system. Make it on a large baseboard using papier mâché to form the landscape. Houses can be made

using small pieces of straw and clay (for wattle and daub) and wood. Stone buildings can be made either with card or Plasticine and decorated to look like stone.

Follow-up
Encourage the children to look at contemporary records, such as the *Domesday Book* and monastery accounts to obtain more information. Parish records from Tudor times may give an indication of life expectancy and causes of early death. (Explain that no Parish records are available from before this period.) Find out about the Black Death and how it affected your area. Often whole villages disappeared because all their inhabitants died of plague. Do any of the Ordnance Survey maps refer to sites as 'deserted village'?

Ask the children to imagine what life would have been like under the feudal system. They could then dramatise a 'day in the life of', for example, a serf, villein's wife, priests and so on.

Links with other curriculum areas

PE
- movement of farm machinery;
- movement of farm animals.

RE
- customs and rituals (cross-cultural);
- the farming year.

English
- examples of rural life from literature, diaries, accounts, journals and poems;
- creative writing;
- dramatic reconstruction of rural life scenes.

Art
- pastoral scenes in paintings;
- use of different mediums of paint, collage and clay for models and drawings;
- visit to gallery or museum.

Food and farming

Geography
- animal husbandry and situation of crops;
- comparing UK farming with another country;
- survey of local shops, markets and industry.

Music
- pastoral songs and rhymes;
- folk music and rural musical traditions such as barn dances.

Technology
- system of food production;
- solving problems in food processes such as environmentally-friendly pest control;
- how tools and machines are made.

Maths
- survey of local shops and data collection;
- packaging – statistics, size, shape and so on;
- measurement of land use for farming locally;
- division of land use in the past.

Science
- types of farming – arable or animal husbandry;
- machines needed;
- animal care and needs;
- organic farming.

Houses and places of worship

Stained-glass windows

Age range
Five to seven.

Group size
Small groups.

What you need
Black sugar paper, white crayon, scissors, adhesive sticks, sheets of coloured tissue paper, cooking oil, pictures for reference.

What to do
Let the children look at examples or pictures of various stained-glass windows and tell them that they are going to make their own windows for the classroom. Ask each child to draw a simple abstract shape on to black sugar paper with a white crayon. Their designs should be fairly simple and able to be divided into parts – it is usually best to start with an abstract design. They should then cut out their shapes and cut out the centre of the shape to leave a frame. They should then cut out small strips of black paper and glue them across the frame to create sections. Finally, they should glue pieces of different coloured tissue paper to the back of the frame and brush them with a thin coating of oil (which makes the paper transparent) and allow them to dry. The finished windows can be stuck on the classroom windows so that the light shines through them.

Follow-up
The children can try experimenting with windows made from different shades of the same colour or make similar designs using coloured sticky paper – these will not be transparent.

Ask the children to make a collection of coloured glass items. As these are often very fragile, the children will begin to understand how precious glass used to be and why it was only used in very grand and solidly constructed buildings.

Discuss with them how glass is made. Was it made the same way in the past? Look at an example of a stained-glass window in a local church – which colours are used most? What material has been used to demarcate the panes?

Old and new kitchens

Age range
Five to nine.

Group size
The whole class and pairs.

What you need
A large picture of an old-fashioned kitchen from the last century (see photocopiable page 106), kitchen photographs from this century, flip chart, pen.

What to do
Give each pair a copy of photocopiable page 106 and ask the class to look very carefully at the picture of the old-fashioned kitchen. Ask them to list all the items in the kitchen. How many of these items are still found in kitchens today? Which items are still found, but are designed differently?

Ask the children to work in pairs and give each pair a photograph and ask them to compare and contrast the two (use pictures from catalogues and magazines.) List the items that have changed.

Follow-up
Choose one kitchen item, for example a fridge, and ask the children to draw pictures of it as it looked in the 1950s and how it looks today. They can use old advertisements from magazines to help them. Some examples are shown on photocopiable pages 104–105.

Photocopy a series of kitchen or kitchenware advertisements from magazines and ask the children to sort them into appliances that are still used and those that are no longer used (old magazines can be obtained quite cheaply from collectors' fairs and jumble sales).

Local survey

Age range
Seven to nine.

Group size
The whole class and small groups.

What you need
A large scale map of the area around your school (one mile radius), clipboards, pencils, a camera (optional).

What to do
Discuss with the children the many people who meet together to worship. Consider how there are many forms of religion and how most religious groups have a building in which to worship. Most children will be familiar with a few different types of religious buildings such as churches, synagogues, mosques, Sikh temples, chapels and so on. Show the children a variety of pictures or slides of such buildings and point out the various architectural features which will help the children to identify these buildings.

Take groups of children on a walk around the area of your school. In order to cover a one mile radius, each group should cover a different area. During the walk the children should note any religious buildings or monuments (for example a village cross or War Memorial) which they come across. They can take photographs of them and make detailed on-site drawings.

Once back in the classroom, each group should plot their findings on to the map so that they have a complete record of all the religious buildings near to the school. The children should then try to find out when each was built and a little bit about the history of each building. They can also look at maps from earlier periods to see if these buildings were marked on them.

Follow-up
The children can write to the people in charge of the buildings to see if it is possible to make a visit to see the inside of the building. If this is possible the visits should again be recorded with drawings and photographs if these are permitted. You may want to concentrate on particular aspects such as windows, decoration and size in order to obtain a more detailed picture.

As a class you could also look at the similarities and differences between various buildings and consider the history of particular groups such as the Quakers and Seventh Day Adventists. Discuss why some religious groups are persecuted for their beliefs.

Period room

Age range
Seven to nine.

Group size
Small groups.

What you need
A collection of magazines, books and gallery postcards featuring period homes and interiors; wallpaper off-cuts, card, paints, felt-tipped pens, small pieces of carpeting, an assortment of fabrics, cardboard boxes, scissors, glue.

What to do
Ask the children to sort through the magazines, books and pictures in order to find pictures of houses and room interiors from different periods. Each group should choose a different period and find examples from this period, for example, Georgian, Early and Late Victorian and so on. Some museums such as the Geffrye Museum (see the Resources section) have exhibits set out in rooms and where possible it would be useful to arrange a class visit. The children will then be able to make site drawings of the exhibits and use these as the basis of their models.

Having researched their chosen period each group should make models of their own rooms in the style of this period. They should make their rooms by cutting away one side of a large cardboard box. They can use the wallpaper and the carpet off-cuts to decorate their rooms and pieces of furniture can be drawn on to card, cut out and mounted on to a card stand (two dimensional). More ambitious groups might like to construct items of furniture as scale models.

Display the rooms in chronological order with labels indicating the historical period, e.g. Tudor/Regency/Early Victorian and so on.

Follow-up
Alternatively, a complete house of, for example, the Victorian period could be made with each group contributing a room to a house. The boxes should be of a uniform size so that they can be glued together.

Younger children might prefer to copy a series of rooms from pictures or exhibits. Making a model of one piece of furniture each should be sufficient to give them a feel for the chosen period.

Older children could research fabric patterns and designs and make a chart of examples.

Islamic tile patterns

Age range
Seven to ten.

Group size
Individuals.

What you need
Pictures of Islamic designs, pens or paints in blues and greens, paper squares, rulers, travel brochures.

What to do
Ask the children to look carefully at the pictures of Islamic designs. Tell them to look at the colours which have been used and the way the designs are in the form of abstract patterns or stylised flower and plant forms. (Humans and animals are never used in Islamic art.)

Having studied the patterns tell the children that they are going to make a huge tiled wall using Islamic designs. Give each child a paper square and tell them to divide it into smaller squares and design a symmetrical pattern. They can then colour their tiles using predominantly blues, greens and turquoises.

Once all the squares have been coloured they can be mounted within a frame so that they form a wall.

Follow-up
Show the children tiles designed by William Morris. How far do the children think he based his ideas on Islamic patterns? Can they find examples of similar patterns around them?

Ask the children to look at travel brochures of European and Asian countries and find photographs of decorated buildings. Can they find out how old the buildings are? Which ones are old and which ones are more modern? The children can cut out the pictures and make them into a collage.

Furniture collage

Age range
Nine to eleven.

Group size
Small groups.

What you need
A collection of magazines featuring period furniture; scissors, glue, card, reference books on antiques and price guides if possible.

What to do
Let the children sort through the magazines to find pictures of period furniture. Each child in the group should look for a different item such as chairs, settees, tables, clocks and so on. When they find pictures the children should cut them out and organise them into sets according to date order and/or into historical periods. They should use the reference books to help them with this. Finally, the children can make a collage of their furniture.

Follow-up
Ask the children to choose different items of furniture and mount them individually on to card. They should label each item as accurately as possible, for example, 'a Chippendale chair from around 1790', and then use the cards to play a sort of 'Antiques Road Show' game. To play this game the children can pretend to be experts. They should pick a card and describe the item and value it, for example, 'A good quality Chippendale chair, in very good condition seat a little worn, value _____ .' – they will need the reference books with the price guides to help them. The children can also invent other versions of the game or alternatively, they can devise an auction catalogue using the computer if possible and run mock auctions using pretend objects.

Links with other curriculum areas

Geography
- regional variation in the type of house construction;
- where houses are sited;
- settlement.

Music
- religious music and composers associated with them;
- music for festivals;
- hymns and home music making.

RE
- rituals and festivals;
- survey of local religious buildings;
- investigation of design features such as minarets, spires, domes, stained glass and so on.

Maths
- measurement of buildings – area, shape and space;
- survey of features by size, shape and pattern.

PE
- movement linked with religious customs;
- drama of nomadic life.

Houses and places of worship

Art
- the designs of houses from different periods – furniture, wallpaper, kitchens and so on;
- patterns in tiles and fabric;
- paintings of houses and religious buildings.

English
- houses in literature and poems;
- discussions on feelings of home;
- understanding and empathy through sharing and discussion of views;
- creative and dramatic writing.

Science
- finding out what building materials are made from;
- safety and durability of buildings;
- the use of water and heat in religious ceremonies.

Technology
- how houses are built and from what materials;
- design improvements;
- how domes, arches, unsupported roofs and tall towers are constructed.

Writing and printing

Wax tablets

Age range
Five to seven.

Group size
Individuals.

What you need
Old candles, small, strong lids from cardboard boxes (for example cheese boxes), a saucepan, a pudding basin, cooker, sharp pencils, photocopiable page 107.

What to do
Explain that writing has changed with each historical period. The Viking alphabet consisted of runes etched on stones or tablets; children can simulate these by making wax tablets and using the alphabet provided on photocopiable page 107.

Put pieces of old candle into a basin and melt them by putting the basin in a saucepan of water and heating the water until the wax melts. When the wax has melted pour it slowly into the box lids. When it has cooled and set, the children can etch runes into the wax tablet using a sharp pencil. Can they write their names in runes?

Follow-up
Ask the children to write out short poems using this script, or perhaps a short extract from a Norse saga. The figures on the photocopiable page can be coloured, cut out and used as stick puppets when the children make up stories involving runes.

Clay tablets

Age range
Five to seven.

Group size
Individuals, working in small groups.

What you need
Clay, rulers or strong pieces of card, rolling pins, thick pencils, clay tools or pointed pieces of dowel, photocopiable page 108.

What to do
Firstly explain that the Egyptians wrote using a form of picture letters called hieroglyphs, impressing the symbols on to clay tablets with writing tools. Then give each child a small lump of clay and ask them to roll it out until it is about 1.5cm thick. They should then cut out a straight-edged tablet shape using the rulers or card as a guide. Each tablet should measure about 8cm square. Having cut out their tablets the children can use the pencils or tools to etch letters into the tablets. If they go wrong, the tablet can be rolled out and re-done

(providing that the clay is still damp). Once the children are satisfied with their tablets they can leave them to dry.

Follow-up
Ask the children to use photocopiable page 108 to write simple words or their names in Egyptian hieroglyphs. Larger tablets could be made so that a whole message is written in hieroglyphs. Ask the children to find out more about Egyptian writing. Once the children have tried out their own hieroglyphs and learned some of them, they could try to decode examples of writing which they find in books about this period.

Personal seal

Age range
Seven to nine.

Group size
Individuals, working in small groups.

What you need
Paper, pencils, pressprint, small pieces of balsa wood (about 8cm in length by 2.5cm × 2.5cm square), sealing wax, candles, Plasticine, small pieces of ribbon.

What to do
In the past, seals were used to make an impression in melted wax. Documents were signed in this way (for example the Great Seal of Magna Carta) and letters were sealed too. This meant that when the recipient received a letter with an unbroken seal, he knew that no-one had meddled with it. Consider with the class just

how important this might be when the only messages that were written were ones of major importance.

Let the children practise designing a simple signature which is distinctive to them. This can be in the form of one initial or several initials inter-twined. Once they have decided on a design they can begin to make their own seals. Ask them to cut their design into the top of the wood by drawing clearly and firmly with a thick pencil. The seal is now ready for use.

Melt the wax for a few seconds over the candle flame and then use one of the children's seals to demonstrate how letters and documents were sealed.

Follow-up
Let the children use the seal as a printing tool and print signatures on pretend letters and documents. They could make Plasticine seals by cutting out a round shape from the Plasticine and fixing a small piece of ribbon to the back of it. These pieces of Plasticine can be impressed by the wood seals. If possible get hold of a signet ring and show how this would have been used in the past.

Quill pen

Age range
Seven to nine.

Group size
Individuals.

What you need
Brown paper, sharp scissors, ink, large feathers from birds such as gulls, geese or crows.

What to do
Explain to the children that they will be making quill pens to simulate past writing practice before the invention of mass-produced nibbed instruments. Tell them that Shakespeare, for example, wrote all his plays with a quill pen. Ask them how difficult do they think it would have been to write legibly? How long would it have taken to write a page and what sort of blotting material would have been needed to prevent smudging?

Tell the children to cut off the end of the feather at an angle and cut a small slit at the point. They can then dip the point in ink and practise writing.

For a parchment effect the children should write on sheets of brown paper. They can write letters and seal them with their seals (see previous activity).

Follow-up
Let the children practise writing out the alphabet on plain white paper. They should try out different scripts and then write a popular motto such as 'A stitch in time saves nine' using the quill pen. Explain that short, well-known phrases have often been used in the past for handwriting practice. They can decorate their mottoes with a decorative border.

Illuminated letters

Age range
Nine to eleven.

Group size
Small groups.

What you need
Pictures of illuminated manuscripts and letters (The British Museum has a good collection), good quality white paper, felt-tipped pens, rulers.

What to do
Ask the children to look carefully at the designs of some old material manuscripts. They should look especially at how some of the capital letters were decorated with pictures within the letter shape, and how patterns edged and surrounded it.

Ask the children to draw a large capital letter in pencil. They should measure their letters to ensure that they are symmetrical, and curve the ends of their letters a little. Once they have got the outline correct they can draw round their letters in black felt-tipped pen and then illustrate them using coloured pens. (Again it is advisable to work in pencil first until the design is satisfactorily completed.)

Old lettering was done with quill pens and coloured inks or with brushes and paint. Similar decorated letters could be produced using inks and paints. More care will be needed as ink and paint are more fluid mediums. Gold paints could be used sparingly for a more authentic look.

Follow-up
Ask the children to consider the amount of time it must have taken to produce a complete book in this way. They might also like to find out where most books of the Middle Ages were produced and kept. How did the advent of printing affect their production?

Old/new writing collection

Age range
All ages.

Group size
The whole class.

What you need
Examples of different styles of writing from the past – picture writing, Gothic lettering and so on; old and new writing implements and materials, a display table, a large piece of material.

What to do
Set up a writing display table to form the focus for the topic. Display on it the children's clay tablets, wax tablets, seals, illuminated lettering and so on. Also collect pictures, postcards and books giving examples of old documents and letters. Perhaps the children will have old letters at home which could also be brought in. Old books, newspapers, postcards and letters can all be picked up cheaply at collectors' fairs.

Try to organise all the examples in date order. Put the newer items on a separate side of the display. Items should include typewriters, a computer, modern books and writing materials. There is a vast number of items which could be included and so you will have to be selective and look only at, for example, forms of print.

Follow-up
Encourage the children to collect as many examples of items connected with writing as possible and find out as much as possible about old writing materials and how they were used. Many people in the past could not read or write and often used to sign their name with a cross. See if you can obtain examples of Victorian certificates from St. Catherine's House (births, marriages and deaths) with cross signatures. Find extracts in old newspapers which refer to illiteracy in any way.

Links with other curriculum areas

Geography
- survey of graphics and advertising in local area;
- travel lines of languages, e.g. Anglo-Saxon roots, words from Indian sub-continent.

Maths
- letter patterns;
- classification of books;
- measurement, numbering and indexing in book making;
- data collection from survey.

Music/PE
- graphic scores;
- choreography;
- printed sheet music.

RE
- importance of literacy;
- information;
- religious writings;
- propaganda;
- place of advertising.

History
- origins of words;
- historical development of scripts and alphabets;
- importance of written documents;
- famous documents e.g. The Magna Carta;
- letters from past periods.

Writing and printing

English
- drama involving development of writing;
- purposes of writing;
- different types of writing collected and done by children:
  - creative writing
  - poems
  records/diary accounts, lists.

Technology
- paper making;
- book making;
- development of print e.g. blocks, printing presses;
- layout of newspapers;
- visit to a printers;
- design and production of newspaper for class;
- inventions:
  - Braille
  - typewriter
  - photocopier
  - fax.

Art
- photographs and illustrations;
- designing advertisements;
- book illustration;
- calligraphy;
- writing implements;
- illuminated letters;
- printing blocks.

Science
- materials used for writing and tools;
- processes involved in printing, e.g.:
  - forces involved in printing presses
  - colour
  - light in photocopying
  - printing, etc.

Land transport

Transport time board

Age range
Five to seven.

Group size
Small groups.

What you need
Large fabric-covered board, strips of Velcro, card, colouring pencils or pens, scissors, glue, pictures of old buses, coaches, cars, bikes, trains and so on.

What to do
Give each group of children a particular form of transport to look at, for example, cars, bikes, trains and so on. Each group should draw about six examples of different types and models. These should be copied carefully from books and magazines (I-Spy books have a good selection). The children should colour their pictures, cut them out and stick them on to card. They should research the dates of their vehicles and write them on the card. Finally, they should fix a piece of Velcro to the back of the card and stick each vehicle to the board.

Let the children move the vehicles around on the board and stick them in time order as far as possible. It should be possible to make a bus time-line, for example, as well as a general time-line from the horse to the car in the present day.

Follow-up
If possible, organise a trip to a transport museum so that the children can experience at firsthand transport in an historical context. Encourage them to look at methods of transport which are no longer used and to examine the reasons for this. Alternatively, invite a visitor to the class who can talk to children about times when trams were common, when trains were powered by steam and so on.

Advertisements old and new

Age range
Six to eight.

Group size
Small groups.

What you need
A collection of recent car advertisements, car advertisements from the 1950s, 1960s and 1970s, paper, pencils.

What to do
Give each group two car advertisements, one old and one modern, and two sheets of paper. One of the sheets should be headed 'similarities', the other 'differences'. Ask the children to choose one member of the group to act as scribe. The children can then compare the advertisements and the scribe should write their comments on the appropriate sheet.

Encourage the children to look at the designs of the cars; the number of illustrations used; whether colour is used; what sort of lettering is used; the type of layout and if possible what the advertisement says. Finally, each group should compare their findings. Do the results tell us anything about who is buying cars now and who used to buy them?

Follow-up
Ask the children to look at examples of old and new advertisements for other products connected with transport. How have these changed? They can also look at old and new styles of packaging or compare the advertisements on buses and stations today with those in pictures from the 1900s. Do any of their local stations still have old advertisements displayed?

Railway drama

Age range
Eight to ten.

Group size
The whole class and small groups.

What you need
Photocopiable pages 109 to 112, reference books about the history of the railway.

What to do
Read to the children some of the accounts of railway building. Discuss with them how this must have been a major engineering project – building tunnels, bridges, viaducts and thousands of miles of track. Encourage

them to think about issues such as the noise and pollution from the steam locomotives and discuss how the railways speeded up travel for ordinary people and enabled freight to be carried more quickly to a wider range of destinations.

Let the children look at photocopiable pages 109 to 111 which give details of how the railway network grew. Many areas in Britain before the railways did not have many visitors as they were difficult to reach by road. However, the building of the railways meant the people could easily reach a lot more places. The improvement of transport also meant that people could commute from the country to work in towns and this led to new homes being built on green field sites.

All these changes meant that people had mixed feelings about the railways when they came. Use photocopiable page 112 which shows a proposal for building a railway line through a small village to enable the children to understand the advantages and disadvantages of these changes. One group of children should take on the roles of the characters and act out their responses as far as they can in role. The rest of the class should listen to the arguments and then add some of their own – again trying to act in role as a person of the period. The class should then decide on whether or not to allow the proposed railway to be built.

Follow-up
Take similar events, such as the invention of the telephone, electric light or new machinery in factories and devise a similar dramatisation enabling children to play different roles and consider different viewpoints.

Canal routes

Age range
Nine to eleven.

Group size
Small groups.

What you need
A local Ordnance Survey map (scale 2cm:1km), photocopiable page 113, reference books about the locality in the eighteenth and nineteenth century.

What to do
Ask the children to colour in the canal routes on photocopiable page 113. Point out to them how the network of canals spans most parts of England and Wales. Can they locate a canal in their area on the map? Now, using a current Ordnance Survey map for the area, can they can locate this canal? It may be marked on the map as 'disused'. If the canal is not still in use, try to trace the old route. Many parts of the canal

may have been filled in, but hopefully it will be possible to make out its original route. See if you can find maps from, say, 1940, 1910 and 1880 of the same area and see whether the children can trace the canal route at an earlier date.

If the children have found a canal in their locality they can try to find out more details about it by looking at local reference books or by contacting the local library/museum. Can they find out when the canal was built? Are there any stories about its construction and use? Canal building, particularly if tunnels were involved, was often a dangerous job and they may be able to find contemporary accounts of accidents or interesting incidents connected with the canal.

Follow-up
Let the children dramatise an incident or write an account of what it must have been like to leg a canal barge through a very long, dark, narrow tunnel.

Pilgrim route

Age range
Nine to eleven.

Group size
Small groups.

What you need
Ordnance Survey maps of south London and Kent (scale 2cm:1km), a copy of Chaucer's *Canterbury Tales* (*The road to Canterbury* (Heinemann 1979) and *The Canterbury Tales* (Longman 1987) are both suitable editions for this age group), art materials.

What to do
Tell the children the story of Chaucer's pilgrimage to Canterbury. Many people during the Middle Ages went on pilgrimages to Canterbury and other religious shrines. Ask the children to trace the route of Chaucer's pilgrims on an Ordnance Survey map. It will be marked as the 'Pilgrims Way', extending from Southwark to Canterbury. Different groups can have different maps and they should draw the route of the journey in their particular area, noting which towns and villages the pilgrims pass through. The whole route can then be transcribed on to a large piece of paper to form the basis of a wall story.

Talk about the main characters who went on Chaucer's pilgrimage and read out their descriptions. The children should then be able to draw and paint them as figures to go on the pilgrim frieze.

Follow-up

Read one or two of the stories and talk about some of the customs and the way of life which they reveal. Ask the children to find out about other places of pilgrimage and customs associated with them, particularly if there are any in your area.

If possible visit the Chaucer Centre at Canterbury. This will provide a wonderful experience for the children of life at that time.

Highwayman's story

Age range
Nine to eleven.

Group size
The whole class.

What you need
Books about the lives of highwaymen such as Dick Turpin; Alfred Noyes's poem 'The Highwayman', paper, pens, camera.

What to do
Read Alfred Noyes's poem 'The Highwayman' (O.U.P. 1981) to the class. Talk about the images it evokes. What does it tell us about how the highwayman feels? Do they think that the people who had been robbed by him would feel so sympathetic? Read other stories about highwaymen and women to the children, particularly ones about Dick Turpin.

Discuss with the children the dangers of travel and the sense of adventure which these stories inspire. Use these stories to spark off creative writing. Encourage a variety of viewpoints and format.

Follow-up
Ask the children to decide on some of the key incidents of the Dick Turpin story or Noyes's poem. They should then set up six scenes and dramatise them using props and costumes as necessary. Photograph each of the scenes as it is being performed. The photographs can then be mounted in a book and the children can write appropriate text to accompany them. This will provide a record of the class work and the children will be able to discuss and analyse the historical accuracy of their dramatisation of events. What are the areas of interpretation? How can the children check these for accuracy?

Links with other curriculum areas

Geography
- canal, rail and road routes;
- old routes – pilgrim paths and so on;
- mapping skills;
- industry supporting transport.

Technology
- development of the wheel;
- how different types of vehicles are made and work;
- design improvements – issues of pollution.

Music
- sounds of transport;
- music associated with transport;
- songs and rhymes.

PE
- movement of different vehicles;
- dramatising events such as highway robbery using a variety of movement.

Land transport

RE
- customs related to travel;
- values and feelings about travel;
- fears – change, robbery and so on.

English
- transport in literature and poems;
- creative writing;
- using local records for information;
- dramatising events from the past, for example the coming of the railway.

Maths
- types of travel – sort into sets;
- surveys of routes;
- local surveys of traffic – number of buses per day;
- data collection based on type of car – size, shape, colour and so on.

Art
- transport in art;
- visual galleries;
- collecting postcards and photographs of transport;
- looking for local pictures of transport.

Science
- steam power, electric power and petrol power;
- how engines work – gears and so on;
- materials used to make vehicles and processes and principles involved;
- horses – care and needs.

Domestic life, families and childhood

Images of childhood

Age range
Five to seven.

Group size
Small groups.

What you need
Magazines which have a variety of pictures of children; scissors, paste, plain paper.

What to do
Give each child a magazine and ask them to find and cut out all the pictures of children that they can find. When they have done this, ask them to sort their pictures into sets. Let the children choose their own categories: they might choose, for example, 'children playing', 'children on their own', 'feeling sad', 'children eating' and so on. Tell them to count the number of images in each category and then tabulate their results. Ask the children why they think there are more images in certain sets. Why do they think the different categories of picture were taken?

Finally, each child can make a collage of the images from a particular category and label their collages with a title such as 'Children advertising food'.

Having looked at current images of childhood ask the children to make a collection of images of childhood from the past. They will have to do this from museum/gallery postcards, old photographs and copies of old magazines (many are cheaply available from the 1940s and 1950s). Photocopy these so that the children can work in groups, categorising and discussing their selections. Tell them to make a similar set of collages with labels and compare them to those of the present listing the main similarities and differences between them. The groups can then pose questions to the rest of the class in order to find out why this might be.

Family tree

Age range
Five to seven.

Group size
The whole class and small groups.

What you need
Sheets of paper, small books, writing and drawing materials, scissors, glue.

What to do
First instigate a class discussion about when the children were babies. Talk about the fact that they have two natural parents — but be sensitive to the fact that the children may not live with their natural parents. The children's families may include step-parents, and/or other relatives or carers. (In doing your research before the activity it is a good idea to talk to parents about this first.)

Ask the children to draw a picture of themselves and their mother and father or main carers on a small piece of paper and, if possible, to name them. Then, talk about grandparents and how each child has two sets. Again, they may not be aware of them, but if they are they should draw them and name them. The children should then mount their pictures on a piece of paper in tree format.

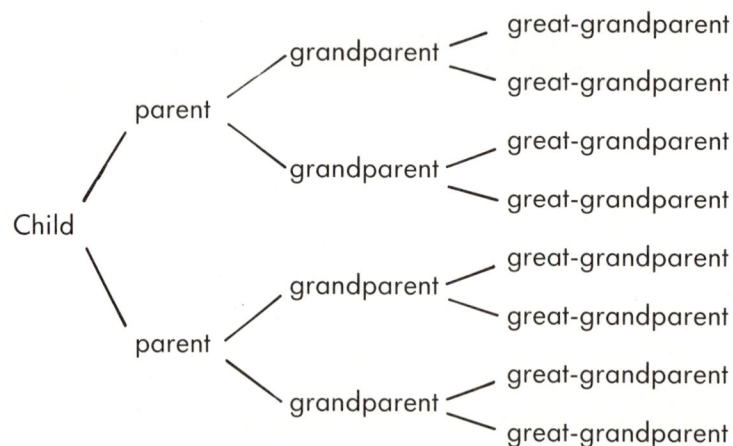

and so on.

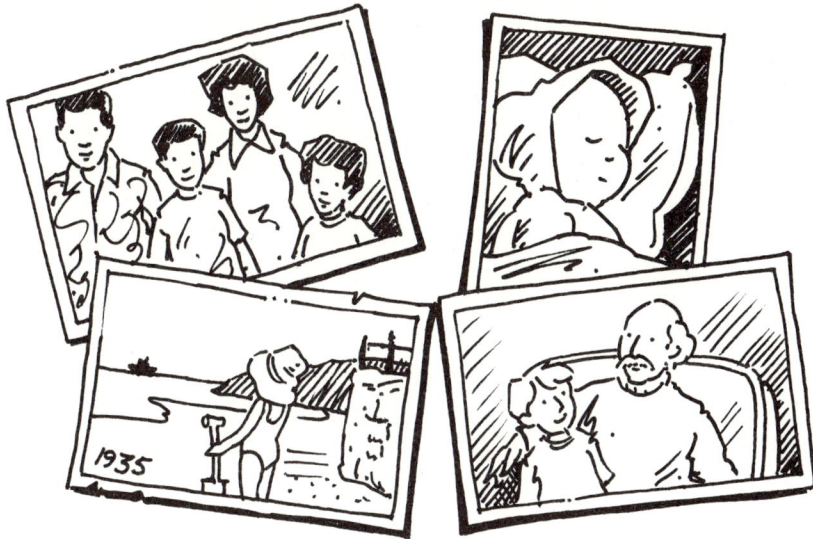

Make little books with the children where they can record the same information. If possible this could also be illustrated with family photographs. It might be possible to discover where parents and grandparents were born. If so, this information could be plotted on local, regional or world maps, both in these books and on a wall chart and statistics about the different places gathered.

Follow-up
Make a class time-line beginning with a fictitious child and leading to parents, grandparents, great-grandparents and great-grandparents and great-great-grandparents. You will need to make this up unless you are able to produce your own!

Alternatively, you could use a well-documented tree like the Queen's as an example. Some children may have access to information which goes even further back and which could be used. Indicate the ways in which it is possible to trace ancestry.

Sequence cards

Age range
Five to seven.

Group size
Small groups.

What you need
A selection of magazines with lots of illustrations; scissors, paste, small pieces of card about 8cm × 5cm.

What to do
Give each group of children a few magazines and pairs of scissors. Ask each group to look through the magazines and cut out a different set of people such as babies, toddlers, schoolchildren, teenagers, adults,

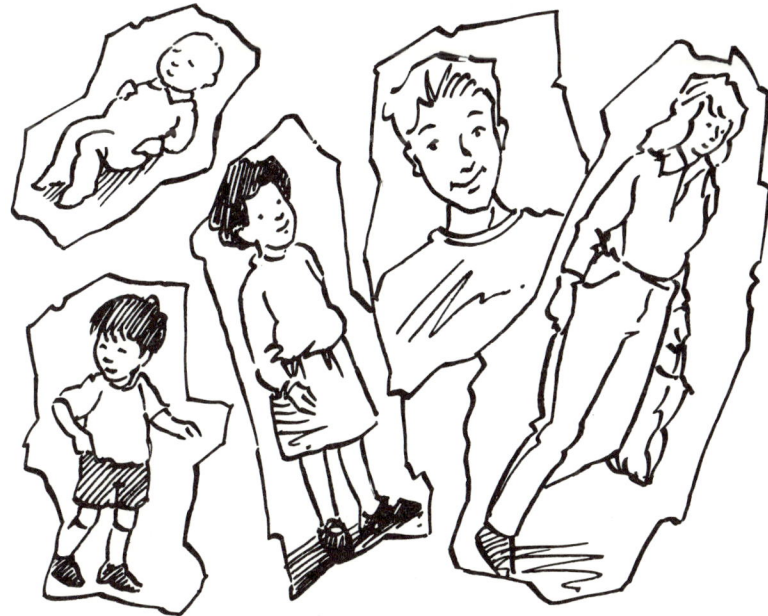

elderly people and so on. Choose as many aged-referenced categories as possible.

The children should stick suitable pictures on cards and the completed cards can be laminated. The children can now use the cards for sequencing – baby to adult. They can also make up their own games and sort them into different sets.

Follow-up
Discuss how we categorise by age. What clues do we use? Size? Clothes? Movement? Is it always possible to categorise by age accurately? Choose some of the pictures at random and play 'Guess the age'. Indicate how easy it is to stereotype people in different age categories and assume their behaviour will all be the same.

Clothes frieze

Age range
Seven to nine.

Group size
Small groups.

What you need
A selection of clothes for different ages and sizes; board for a frieze.

What to do
Ask the children to bring in, with permission, any old clothes that they have belonging to any member of their family. If this proves difficult a selection can be bought quite cheaply from charity shops. You should aim for

quite a large selection of type and size of clothes. Ask one group of children to sort out the clothes by size. Another group can record this information in sets, for example 'We found four baby's dresses' and so on. A third group can choose an item from each set to indicate the size/type of clothes worn from babyhood to adulthood.

Finally, the children can display the clothes as a time-line indicating the ages of the people who would wear them, for example, clothes worn by a baby under one, a baby aged one to two, a five year old, a seven year old, a fifteen year old and so on. The more you can subdivide the better.

Follow-up
Ask the children to draw the time-line in their books and illustrate them with photographs of themselves from babyhood.

A similar time-line could be made if you are able to get clothes from previous decades. If the actual clothes are not available, photographs could be used instead.

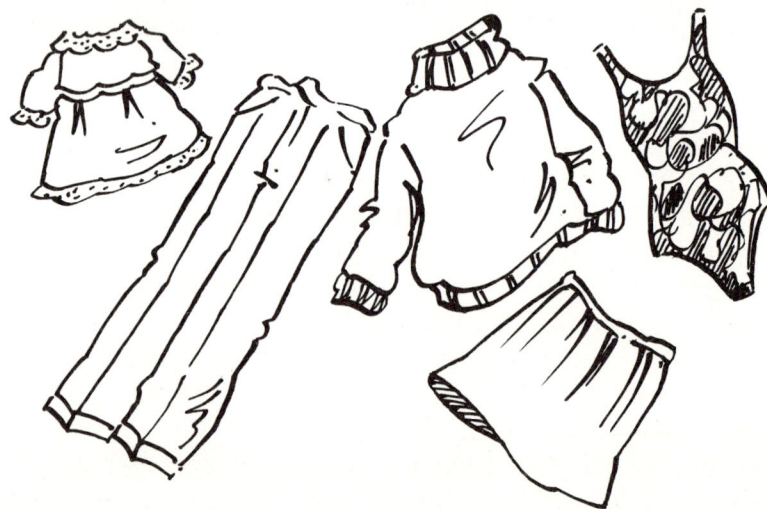

Story of a marriage

Age range
Nine to eleven.

Group size
Pairs.

What you need
Photocopiable page 114, paper, pens.

What to do
Organise the children into pairs and give each pair a copy of the marriage certificate on photocopiable page 114. Ask the children to look at the certificate carefully and write down as much information as possible that they can find out from it. Ask them to imagine that they are writing a report for the local newspaper about the wedding and use this information to write a story about the marriage. They could suggest that the couple had run away from home, that no guests had turned up at the reception, the bride was late having been lost in the fog and so on. The clues that they use to make up their story should centre around such details as the age of the couple and so on. The children should make sure that their stories are realistic, simply adding another dimension to the bare details of the certificate.

Follow-up
The children's stories can be illustrated and mounted into a class book. The class can choose various versions and act them out. They should discuss how realistic each story is and whether it fits the facts that they know. Find an example of a wedding report from an earlier time and ask the children to compare it with a recent one. Does each report contain a similar account of detail? Which is the more interesting to read?

Your school then and now

Age range
Nine to eleven.

Group size
The whole class and small groups.

What you need
Photographs of your school from the past, old school log books, old text books or exercise books, old material relating to the curriculum, old concert or sports day programmes, recent photographs of the school, recent text books, computer with data base software (optional).

What to do
Some of the old material relating to your school may be readily available but if not try contacting your local library and record office to see if they have any information about your school.

Organise the class into groups to give each group a particular aspect of school life to look at. For example, one group could look at the way the building has changed, comparing old photos of the exterior with today's, while other groups could look at the classrooms, or compare particular events. If the school is a modern building the children should try to find out what was built on the site before their school. Alternatively, they could look at where children of the area went to school before their new school was built.

If you have log books, the children can analyse them for information about discipline, attendance, the number of staff and so on. Also an interesting comparison between the reading books used in the past and the ones used today could be done. In all cases the aim should be to consider the similarities and differences between schooling today and in the past, and to record this information. If you have a computer and data base software the children can use this to compile a data base.

Follow-up
Ask the children to put in chronological order events in the school's history. If you find old text books or lesson syllabi you can use them to devise lessons in, for example, the Victorian style, or in the style of the 1920s. You might also like to consider dressing up in clothes similar to school clothes of the past.

Discuss with the children and let them write about punishments and behaviour. Similarly, discuss any records relating to the health of past school children and the need for school meals, rests for young children, fresh air (some schools were built with special verandas) and so on. What does the design of your school tell you about the architect's intentions?

Links with other curriculum areas

PE
- movement connected with growth and change.

RE
- customs, festivals and religions;
- child-rearing patterns.

Geography
- regional differences in life patterns;
- comparisons with Europe.

Music
- music for festivals such as carols;
- songs and rhymes about families and children.

Domestic life, families and childhood

Technology
- improving home design;
- toy design and manufacture;
- how kitchen gadgets work.

Art
- recording by painting, drawing, collages, models and so on;
- families and children shown in art;
- design of homes – interiors and exteriors;
- hobbies.

English
- excerpts from literature and poems;
- written accounts, diaries, oral history;
- making notes, recording, creative writing, interviews and discussion.

Science
- building materials used in the past and how they affected lifestyles;
- domestic inventions – washing machines etc.
- domestic industry e.g. weaving.

Maths
- sorting and sets of family history work;
- sequencing and measuring time;
- surveys about family life in the past – data collection.

Local history

Shop survey

Age range
Five to seven.

Group size
Small groups.

What you need
Clipboards, pencils, camera, adult helpers to accompany visit, tape recorders.

What to do
Choose a row of local shops to investigate. A number of visits will need to be made. First one group of children should make a photographic record of the shops. These should then be displayed in order as a street scene. Other groups of children can then interview the various shop-keepers about their shops in the past. They should prepare a list of interview questions in advance, such as 'How long have you run the shop?' 'Who was here before you?' 'When was it built?' 'Was it always a butchers?' and so on. The children can then write a short informative piece about each shop.

Follow-up
If the row of shops is old, it should be possible to look up information about them using trade directories or if the shops are Victorian, in Post Office Directories such as Kelly's. It should then be possible to see how the shops have changed hands, merchandise and so on.

Some shops may have been passed down through two or more generations of a family. The 1891 census may also provide useful information and the children can also check old newspapers and directories for advertisements which may feature the shops.

The photographic street scene could be illustrated by close observational drawings and/or clay pictures. Use the photographs for reference.

Churchyard investigation

Age range
Six to eleven.

Group size
Small groups.

What you need
Clipboards, pencils, camera (optional), adult helpers to accompany visit.

What to do
Churchyards contain a lot of information about life in the past. Talk with the children about the way details may be recorded on grave stones and monuments – explain how to look for ages, dates and so on. Some monumental inscriptions give further information in the form of short poems or stories. Deal with this issue sensitively as some children may recently have experienced bereavement. You should also discuss some of the different views people might have about

death and burial, both religious and secular. It may also be important to allay fears about visiting a place which is so often an element in stories of the macabre.

Divide the class into groups for the visit to a local church. Each group can visit a different section of the churchyard, systematically recording inscriptions, or recording particular details, such as a list of names, types of stone and so on. The children should write down descriptions together with any on-site drawings and if possible take photographs too.

The scale of the investigation will depend very much on the size of the area involved. If this is large, it might be best to get the children to make detailed notes about

only one or two monuments each. Some areas may have cemeteries which were built in Victorian times. There is usually local information about the most interesting monuments to be seen in them and you might want to use this as the basis for your investigation.

Once back in the classroom the children should work together in their groups to record and analyse their information. What is the most common female name they found? What was the oldest age of death they found?

History of our homes

Age range
Seven to nine.

Group size
The whole class and individuals.

What you need
Details of where the children live, local newspapers, list of local estate agents, copies of a map of the area where children live, paper, pens.

What to do
Fix a large detailed map of the area on the wall at child height. Mark on it all the children's addresses. Make a list of all the roads where the children live and mount this information next to the map.

Ask each child to guess how old their homes are. Record this information and mount it alongside the map, indicating any reasons why they think this should be the case. The children should now try to find out when their homes were really built. They should check the estate

agents columns in the local paper. This may list similar homes in the same street with an approximate age. The children can also write to a local estate agent for information about when their home was built. For homes that were built by the local authority, the children should write to their local housing department for information.

Once the children have dated their homes this information should be recorded alongside the children's original guesses. How different are the two sets of dates? Was anyone very close? Anyone wildly out? Discuss further some of the clues that might be used to date buildings – style, architecture and so on.

Follow-up

Ask the children to either take photographs of their homes or to draw pictures of them. These pictures can be mounted and displayed in date order. See how many houses were built around the same time. Can the children find out why this is? (Building of the local railway, end of the war and so on.) The children can use local reference books to find out about key local events in order to give them this background information.

Other streets may have names like Boskins Row and these are likely to commemorate more locally famous people. Are there any streets that could fit into this category in your area?

Take groups of children for walks around the local area and tell them to record any statues or plaques which also record notables. You may find foundation stones on chapels, schools and public buildings and objects such as cattle troughs and seats may also have

Local characters

Age range
Seven to nine.

Group size
Small groups.

What you need
Clipboards, pencils, camera, adult helpers to accompany visit, local street map, local reference books.

What to do
Let the children look at a local street map. Discuss the names of roads. Are there any roads which have names like Albert Road, Nightingale Lane, Gordon Street, Browning Terrace? If so, these may well commemorate famous Victorians and have been built around that time. Ask the children to find out about some of these people and write about their lives. Why were they so famous?

inscriptions. Let the children photograph or draw these things and then try to find out about these local people and what they contributed to the community.

Follow-up
Sometimes plaques record the visit of a celebrity or member of the Royal Family. Ask the children to try and find accounts of the events in old newspapers and write a short piece about them. Who is asked to open buildings today? Would Royalty and celebrities still be invited? Has our idea of who is famous and who is important changed? What evidence from this survey might lead the children to draw such conclusions?

Newspaper extract

Age range
Eight to eleven.

Group size
Small groups.

What you need
Photocopiable page 115, paper, pens.

What to do
Ask the children to read their extracts in their groups and, having chosen a particular story, decide upon its main features. What happened? Who was involved? How much detail is given? Does the reporter express any opinion? How do the children feel about what happened? What are their opinions? Tell each group to write down their findings. They should then relay this information to the rest of the class and discuss any differences in the groups comments.

Is it possible to record events objectively? Do we all see an event in the same way? Set up a short dramatic scene with a few children involved in the action. The rest of the class should act as witnesses to the event. Each child must then write an account of what they have seen. This should be done immediately after the event and each child should write without any discussion with anyone else. The actors should also write their versions of the event. The accounts should be completed quickly and handed in.

After a week has elapsed ask the class to write a second report of the event. When they have done this hand them back their first reports. In pairs, the children should read each other's reports and make a list of the differences between their first and second reports. When they find differences they should question their partners about why this is so.

The information can then be fed back to the whole class, who should discuss some of the reasons for them: loss of memory; influenced by someone else after discussion and so on. Draw attention to the fact that many reports are written a long time after the event which may mean that they are not totally accurate. Discuss the variety of views expressed and how truth differs with interpretation.

Follow-up
Similar role play exercises and discussion of reported events in the papers and on television will help to reinforce these concepts.

Comparing maps

Age range
Eight to eleven.

Group size
Small groups.

What you need
Maps of your area from several periods such as 1910, 1950, 1890, 1870, 1840, 1700 (see your local library); paper, pens, pencils, a current map of the area.

What to do
Before you begin this activity the children will need to do some preliminary work on looking at map symbols, how to read a map and so on. Try to obtain a number of local maps from different periods and as near as possible to the same scale. Divide the maps into sections and photocopy the same section from each map for each group. Each group will then have a set of sections

covering the same area over several periods. Ask the children to arrange their maps in date order starting with one from the earliest period. What can they see when they've done this? Are the same features still shown on the next map in the sequence? Are new features shown? The children should also compare the later maps for changes.

Once each group has examined their sections they should share their information with the rest of the class. It should be possible to note changes like new roads, railways and housing while many boundaries and open spaces will probably have remained relatively unchanged.

Follow-up
Ask the children to record some of the information that they discover either in chart form or on a data base. For example, they could note the number of open spaces in 1890, 1950 and 1990. Can they record when their school first appeared on the map. How many churches were there in 1840 and 1910?

54

Links with other curriculum areas

PE
- movement (and drama) inspired by a local event.

RE
- survey of local places of worship;
- history of their development;
- local customs and traditions;
- visit to local churchyards and churches.

Art
- looking at local architecture;
- visiting local galleries and artists;
- recording local sites using close observation – painting, modelling, photography and so on.

Maths
- data collection based on local surveys;
- architecture – shape and number of windows, doors, pattern of brick work and so on;
- shopping survey.

Local history

English
- using local oral histories and local records;
- recording interviews;
- local diaries and accounts;
- using libraries and archives;
- dramatising the lives of local people;
- looking at local literature;
- creative writing about past local events.

Music
- listening to local choirs and orchestras and finding out about when they started and so on;
- finding out about local music.

Geography
- site of settlement;
- geological features;
- industry and shops – economic situation compared with towns or villages in Europe;
- how the area has changed – looking at local maps.

Technology
- how things work such as the town clock;
- local environment – litter, pollution, improving facilities;
- changes since the Industrial Revolution.

Science
- community health – local boards, past epidemics, death rate, infant mortality and so on;
- survey of doctors, clinics and so on.

Looking at history through non-history themes

Ourselves

Sharing circle

Age range
Five to seven.

Group size
The whole class.

What you need
An old artefact, large sheet of paper, thick felt-tipped pen.

What to do
Sit with the children in a circle on a carpeted area. Position yourself so that you have a large piece of paper in front of you which the children are able to see you write on. Explain to the children that you are going to pass around an object and each child must make an observation about it. Every comment is valid and you should remind them to think about shape, size, colour, material, hardness, texture, use, manufacture, similarities and differences to other objects and so on. The idea is to encourage the children to take turns, listen to each other, appreciate other viewpoints and consider ideas, as well as encouraging close observational skills as a means of finding out about the past.

Make a note of each child's comment on the large sheet of paper as the artefact is passed round. Read them through from time to time to remind the children of what has been said and encourage new thoughts. This activity may take some time as the children will need to think carefully before speaking. If a child is very slow, move on, but ensure that you return. Go round all the children twice until everyone has exhausted their thoughts. Record the comments exactly as they are spoken so that you capture the language used.

Follow-up
Record the children's comments in a book alongside individual drawings and paintings of the artefact. Display the original sheet of comments on the wall for reference. In groups the children can examine the artefact again and write about it. Many of the words they need will be on the comment sheet. They chould check reference books for further information.

This activity will foster empathy for the past and encourage the children to respect each other's interpretations, a necessary preliminary to understanding how evidence is viewed in different ways.

Old hats

Age range
Five to seven.

Group size
Groups of four.

What you need
A collection of old hats, mirror, tape recorder, large sheets of paper, drawing-pins, thick felt-tipped pens, camera.

What to do
Set up the hats in a corner of the room with a mirror and a tape recorder. As there will be a certain amount of noisy role play make sure that you site this area well away from quiet work! Ask the children to take turns to wear the hats and invent roles. They should record on the tape recorder who they are when wearing the different hats. This role-playing encourages an empathy with people in the past and stimulates the children's imagination. If possible take some photos of the children in role.

Pin a sheet of paper on the wall and write the children's names on it, together with a drawing of each hat. As the children play they should write on the chart who they were when wearing each hat. After they have had a reasonable play with all the hats ask them to express a preference for a particular hat. Record this information on another sheet of paper and take photos of the children in their favourite hat.

Mount the 'favourite hat' photos in a zigzag book. Ask each child to write a short piece underneath their photo about why it was their favourite. As their reasons may have something to do with the role, they should refer back to the recorded information sheets.

Follow-up
Discuss the information gathered with the whole class. What was the most popular role? Are there any obvious gender differences? Are they influenced by television, stories or family roles? Do they like particular hats because of the material or colour?

Child of the past

Age range
Nine to eleven.

Group size
The whole class and small groups.

What you need
Stories, poems and extracts about childhood in the past; access, if possible, to local museums/archives. (It may be possible to invite local achivists or historians to talk to your class about finding evidence.)

What to do

Discuss with the children how life for children used to be very different from how it is today. The concept of childhood is a comparatively recent one and until children went to school on a regular basis they were involved in the normal world of work alongside their parents.

Ask each group to choose a particular period such as Greek, Norman, Tudor, Georgian, 1920s and so on. They sould then find out what the life of a child would have been like during that period. Encourage the children to ask their own questions but if they need a starting point ask them to consider clothing, education, leisure activities and so on. They will probably have to use secondary sources. Is it possible to find out about such details of the past from firsthand evidence?

Tell each group to write and illustrate their findings and then these can be put together into a class book in chronological order. Discuss with the children the importance of always keeping an open mind when using reference books. Encourage them to seek firsthand evidence where possible and ask the question 'How do we know?' They should be satisfied that the facts they have collected are based on sound evidence and aware that facts are subject to interpretation.

Memory book

Age range
All ages.

Group size
The whole class.

What you need
Extracts from stories and poems about childhood memories; paper, pens or pencils.

What to do
Read some extracts of stories and poems that are about memories: try to include a mix of styles and some funny and some sad. Discuss with the children some of their earliest memories. List these on a large sheet of paper and categorise them according to whether they are happy, sad, exciting, shocking and so on. Encourage the children to write about these memories in either prose or poem format. The youngest children might like to record their memories on tape.

Follow-up

Ask the other classes about their memories as well as members of staff and parents. Are most people's memories of childhood happy or sad? Ask the children to write these memories down and use them to make an 'Early memory book'. Alternatively, they could make an 'Early memory tape'. Older juniors might like to video a series of class interviews about memories, but make sure you allow time for editing.

Artefact story

Age range
All ages.

Group size
Small groups.

What you need
A collection of old artefacts such as old books, newspapers, toys, clothes and so on.

What to do
Give each group several old items. These items should not be valuable and should be easily replaceable. Even so, express upon the children the scarce and fragile nature of the items and the need for them to be handled with great care. Items might include an old book, newspapers, magazines, old toys, dolls, a glove, hat, old necklace, pair of glasses, piece of pottery, kitchen grater, a matchbox, old letter, ration book and so on.

Ask each group to look carefully at the objects and to decide what some of them are and how they were used. They should then invent a story about each of the artefacts. Younger children may need a story prompt such as 'These items were left on the bus . . . where do you think the owner was going?' or 'Tell me about the person who owned these'.

When each group has decided on their story they should act it out to the rest of the class.

Suggest ways of finding out more information about the items and show how there are many ways to look at evidence. Archaeologists are often faced with the task of finding artefacts and having to interpret the lives of the people who used them. New evidence often causes them to rethink.

Follow-up

Adjust the objects and groups and repeat the activity. How do the stories now differ? Build up a record of the groups' work by tape recording the plays and using them as reference. In this way you will be able to consider different interpretations of the same evidence.

History from non-history themes

Families
- history of:
  - birthplace
  - names
  - tree of ancestors
- occupations.

Homes
- age of;
- history of;
- local area – parks etc;
- recreation facilities.

School
- when built;
- curriculum;
- discipline;
  - now
  - in the past
- materials used;
- time table in the past;
- private tutors.

Customs
- patterns of birth, marriage and death.

Ourselves

Pets
- origins of types and breeds;
- how transported, e.g. canaries, tortoises;
- famous cats and dogs in history;
- horses in history.

Friends
- childhood in the past;
- leisure/hobbies;
- toys;
- books read in the past.

The environment

Pomander

Age range
Five to seven.

Group size
Pairs.

What you need
An orange for each pair, cloves, a ribbon for each orange.

What to do
Discuss how in the past people did not have the same drainage and sanitation system that we have today. Water closets and piped water were not features of homes until Victorian times. Similarly, until then rubbish and sewage was carried away by open rather than underground drains. Thus the streets were dirty and smelly. In order to counteract some of the unpleasant smells people carried with them posies of sweet-smelling flowers and pomanders. They used flower petals in pot-pourri to scent their homes, and lavender bags to scent linen and clothes.

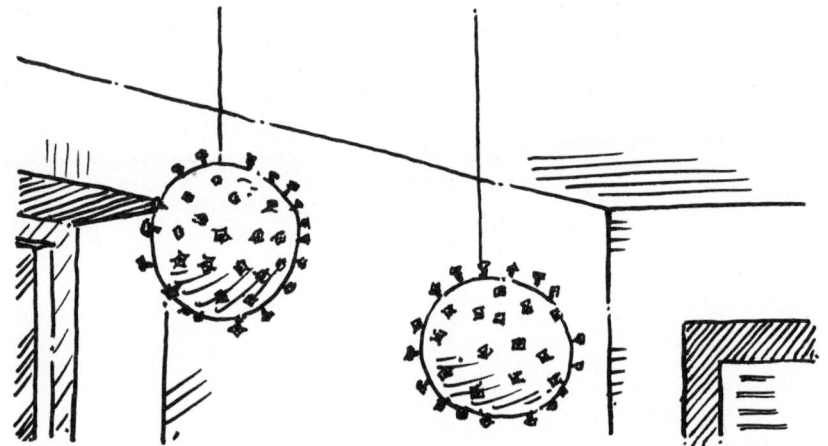

Tell the children that they are going to make their own pomanders. Give each pair of children an orange and ask them to stick the cloves into it until the whole surface is covered. If the children find the cloves difficult to stick into the peel they can make holes in the orange first using a sharp pencil.

Once the oranges have been covered with cloves they should be left to dry in a warm place for a week or two. When the oranges have dried completely the pomander can be decorated by tying a ribbon around it and making a loop at the top so that it can be hung up.

Follow-up
Discuss why spices and herbs were used in this way and how they were also used to disguise food that was not very fresh.

Bridge designs

Age range
Seven to nine.

Group size
The whole class, small groups and pairs.

What you need
Reference books about bridges, paper, pens, art materials, junk materials.

What to do
Look with the children at the types of bridges which were common in different periods. Ask the class to work in groups to find out as much information as they can about particular types of bridges such as clapper bridges, packhorse bridges, drawbridges, suspension bridges and so on. What were they built from? Who invented them? How strong were they? When was this type of bridge first used?

Ask the children to draw each type of bridge clearly and these can then be used to make a wall display. They should be mounted in a time-line with all the information which the children found out written beneath.

Ask each group to choose a different type of bridge and construct a model of it from junk materials. The children can work in pairs and they should try to make them work as fully as possible if this is required. They could also test the strength of their bridges by placing building bricks on top in the middle part of their bridge. How many bricks can it withstand before it collapses?

Follow-up
Can the children think of examples of various types of bridges near to where they live? Try to find out where your nearest bridge is and what type it is. What type of bridge is most common in your area?

Surnames

Age range
Seven to nine.

Group size
The whole class and individuals.

What you need
Reference books about surnames, flip chart and pen or chalkboard.

What to do
Discuss with the children different occupations and trades. Make a list on the board of as many as possible, for example, weaver, thatcher, blacksmith, carpenter, tailor and so on. Ask the children to consider how many

of these trades are also surnames. Tell them that other surnames have derived from place names – again list some of these, hill, forest, river, dale and so on – while some peope were named after towns and villages or after their fathers – Johnson, Peterson, O'Grady.

There are many such examples in other countries as well as England. Non-English names can be analysed in much the same way, but you will need to use bilingual reference books for the purpose or enlist the help of parents and community members.

Ask each child to write down their own surname and think of all the possibilities of from where it derives. They should then check their names in an appropriate reference book to find the real derivation. The children can then design a coat of arms for their family name based on its meaning.

Follow-up
Let the children look through a telephone directory and see how may trade/occupation names they can find. What are the most common surnames? The children might also like to investigate how many other people there are in the directory who have the same name as they do.

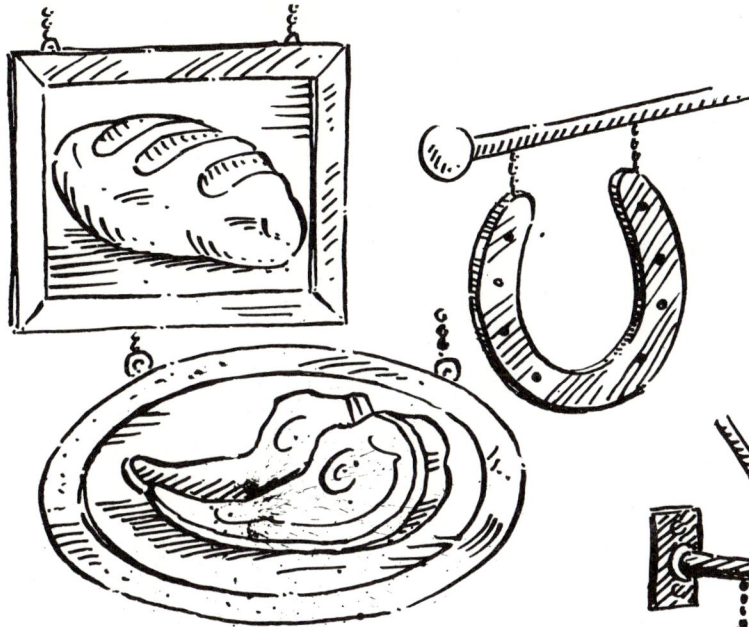

of trades and crafts to each group and ask the children to choose a trade and devise a clear pictorial sign which could hang outside a shop. They should fill their sheets of paper with their designs, illustrating them boldly with paints.

When the signs have been completed hang them up in the classroom making two holes in the top of the sign and threading string through them or by rolling the top of the paper around a thin piece of dowelling.

Follow-up
Suggest that the children design similar signs for contemporary shops and supermarkets. Ask the class to decide upon the most effective design and discuss why.

Shop signs

Age range
Seven to nine.

Group size
Small groups.

What you need
Reference books about crafts and shops, good quality white paper, pencils, paints, string or dowelling.

What to do
In the past many people could not read. Shops therefore displayed their wares under a sign which had a picture on it that indicated their craft – for example a glove for a glove maker or a loaf of bread for a baker. Give a list

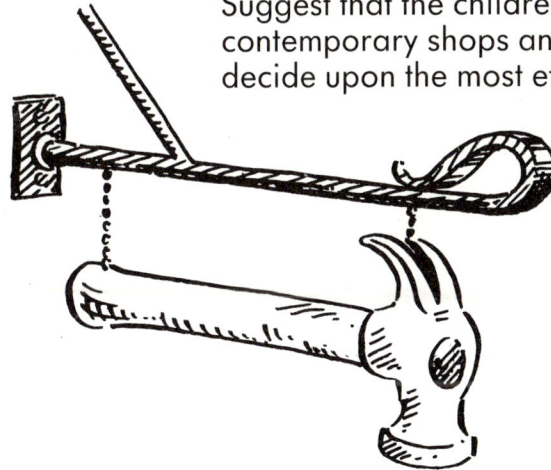

Street furniture

Age range
Nine to eleven.

Group size
Small groups.

What you need
Clipboards, pens, pencils, reference books on the Victorians (particularly local ones with old photos), photocopiable page 116.

What to do
Let the children look at the reference books in small groups. Ask them to pay particular attention to street signs, pillar-boxes, lamp-posts and so on. (I-Spy's *In the Street* is a useful book.) Organise a town trail and ask the children to record all the street furniture that they see by drawing it. A copy of photocopiable page 116 may help each child to find what they are meant to be looking for. Different groups can be taken on walks around different areas if you wish and the children should try to find as many different examples as possible.

Once back in the classroom the children can check their drawings against ones in reference books. How many objects have they found that are Victorian? Award points for anything Victorian which the children have found such as a pillar-box or something even older such as a mounting block, as these items are quite hard to find nowadays.

Follow-up
Ask the children to design their own 'I-Spy' books with pictures of street furniture and points for all the items which are found. The children will need to write a short description of each object and draw a picture of it. The pages could be photocopied or printed and made up into little books for other classes to use. Award the person who gets the most points a title such as 'Street detective of the year'.

The Great Fire of London

Age range
Nine to eleven.

Group size
The whole class.

What you need
Stories about the Great Fire including accounts from Samuel Pepys and John Evelyn; paper, pens.

What to do
Read to the children the accounts of the Great Fire that were written by contemporary diarists. Talk about some of the key information that they supply, for example the date of the fire, where and how it started, how it spread, how people tried to prevent it and its effects. Then let the children read some of the reference books. Is the information they give about the fire the same? Explain to the children how important it is to use firsthand accounts of events as they not only provide evidence, but also often provide personal details and feelings about an event.

Talk about how Pepys and Evelyn felt about the fire. How would the children have felt if they had been there during the fire? Ask them to write a poem indicating how they would have felt as the fire engulfed their homes? They can decorate their finished poems with borders showing drawings of flames.

Follow-up
Discuss the flammability of building materials. Talk about the most likely materials to survive fire. Why were so many buildings in the past made from wood? Let the children investigate the firefighting methods used in the Great Fire and subsequent improvements. How might we prevent a similar tragedy today?

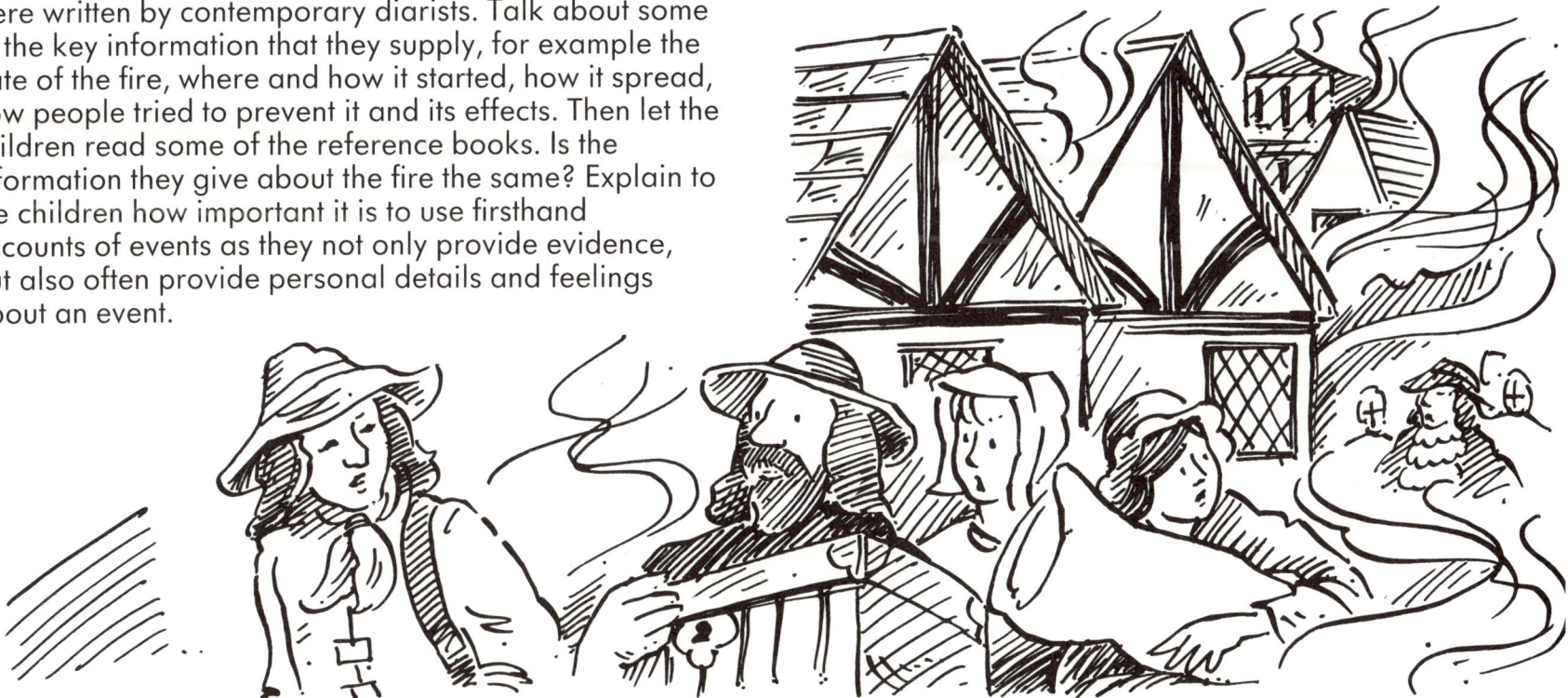

History from non-history themes

Local features
- history of;
- rivers;
- islands;
- harbours;
- hills.

Pollution
- litter;
- drains;
- refuse collection;
- sewage.

Open space
- animals;
- arable farming;
- forest/wooded;
- commons;
- parks;
- local flora and fauna;
- naturalists e.g. Gilbert White.

Transport
- canals;
- roads;
- rail;
- air;
- bridges;
- tunnels;
- stations;
- ports.

The environment

Schools
- date when built;
- changes/extensions;
- history of catchment area.

Housing
- types/variety;
- when built.

Religious buildings
- different religions.

Public buildings
- baths;
- libraries, etc.

Responsibility
- local boards;
- councils;
- Government;
- local dignitaries e.g. Joseph Chamberlain, Birmingham.

Materials

Old toys

Age range
Five to seven.

Group size
The whole class.

What you need
A collection of old toys, several large sheets of paper, a thick felt-tipped pen.

What to do
Ask the children to bring in an old toy, if possible, a toy which belonged to their parents. You will need to stress how precious these toys are and how great care should be taken of them. Make your own collection of toys from antique fairs and sales.

Sit together with the children in a circle on a carpeted area and put all the toys in the centre of the circle so that they are out of reach. Discuss some of the materials which the toys are made from, such as metal, wood and plastic and write these at the top of some large sheets of paper. Place these sheets on the floor next to the toys and ask each child to choose a toy, decide from what it is made and place it on the correct sheet. (You can provide sheets with overlapping sets (e.g. wood and plastic) if necessary.) Continue round the circle until all the toys have been sorted.

Can the children make any observations on their sorting? Are there more very old toys made from metal than newer ones? Discuss how new materials have been introduced, such as plastic.

Follow-up
Borrow the toys for as long as possible so that you can display them. Set up an interactive display whereby the children try to sort them into order of age. If this is not possible, they should sort them into old/very old/new categories.

Pargetting patterns

Age range
Five to eight.

Group size
Groups of four.

What you need
Finger paints, paper for prints, card combs, photocopiable page 117.

What to do
Pargetting or page work is decoration made from moulded plaster featuring on the outside of houses. Sometimes it appears in the form of abstract patterns which are drawn into the wet plaster. Tell the children that they are going to recreate some of these patterns in the classroom.

Tell the children to spread out finger paint fairly thickly on to an art table. then, ask them to use a card comb and to make one of the patterns that is shown on photocopiable page 117. Once they have made their patterns they should lay a sheet of plain paper over the top to take a print. The paint can then be re-used for another pattern.

Follow-up
The children could make similar patterns on plaster of Paris blocks. Tell them to pour the wet plaster of Paris into a mould such as a biscuit tin lid and let it dry. Just before it sets solid they can etch a pattern on to the plaster using a steel comb. This is less easy to do since the plaster must be at just the right consistency for it to work.

Fabric frame

Age range
Six to eight.

Group size
Pairs.

What you need
A selection of photograph frames made from different materials such as plastic, silver, wood, brass, cloth and so on; pieces of fabric, thick cardboard, strong scissors, glue, ruler.

What to do
Ask each child to bring in a photo that they would like to have framed. Also ask them, if possible, to bring in oddments of fabric – cotton fabric with a small pattern is ideal. Make sure you have enough fabric for each child.

1. Back card. Front card. Cut this one out.

Take 2 pieces of card. Draw 2 rectangles on the front piece of card, one 1cm smaller than the other. Cut this one out.

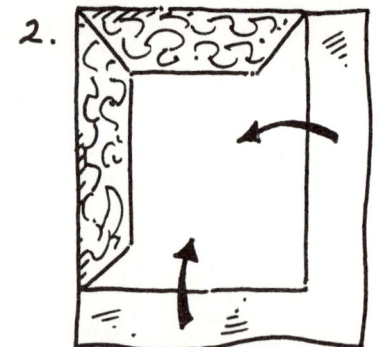

2. Cover back piece of card with material.

Discuss all the different styles of photograph frame there are and show the children some examples. Explain to them that a lot of Victorian frames were made of fabric, as they liked decorative frames. Tell the children that they are going to make their own 'Victorian' picture frames. Give each child two pieces of card – one for the back, the other for the front. Tell them to draw round their photograph on to the card for the front and then draw another rectangle inside this area but about 1cm smaller. They should then cut out the smaller shape.

Tell the children to place the piece of card for the back on the back of the material and draw round it but make it about 2cm bigger than the card. Tell them to cut out the shape and then cover the back piece of card by folding the extra material around the card and sticking it down with glue. They should then do the same with the other piece of card for the front, but this time cut out a window in the middle. To avoid fraying edges, they could cut two diagonal lines across the 'window' and

then fold back and glue the triangular flaps for a neater finish. Finally, they should stick both pieces of card together along three edges but keeping the top open. They can then insert the photograph into the frame. To make a stand for the frame the children should cut a piece of card slightly smaller than the height of the frame, about 4cm wide. This strip should then be narrowed to about 3cm at one end. This end should be folded over and glued to the back of the frame. If the children work in pairs they should require less support from you.

Follow-up
The children can make an attractive classroom display with their frames alongside a selection of other types of frame.

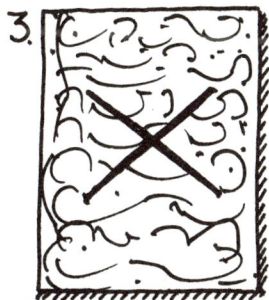

3. Cover front piece of card with material. Cut two diagonals across the material, to make a window in the middle.

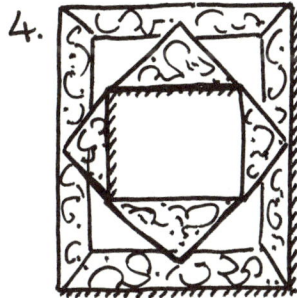

4. Glue back triangular flaps for a neater finish.

5. Do not glue here

Glue the back piece of card to the front piece of card on three sides, leaving the top free to slide in the photograph.

6. Fold here and glue to back of frame

Insert photograph through the slit in the top. Glue a card stand to the back of the frame.

flat-topped piece of triangular card.

Clothing fabric

Age range
Six to eight.

Group size
The whole class and small groups.

What you need
Oddments of different sorts of fabric, reference books on fabrics and costumes, paper, glue, pencils.

What to do
Discuss with the children the clothes they are wearing. How many types of material can they list? Make a word bank for future use.

Give groups of children a collection of fabric scraps. Ask them to sort them out according to the type of fabric, for example a set of velvet pieces, and to stick pieces of fabric in sets on to paper. Select some of the sheets to put up on the wall under the heading 'Materials used for clothes today'.

Let the children read about clothes and costumes in the past. Ask them to investigate the types of fabric that were used. They could look at pictures of the sort of clothes worn by Queen Elizabeth I and make drawings of the elaborately decorated fabric. Ask them to compare this to the clothes a farmer's wife would have worn in the same period.

If possible, organise a visit to a museum to look at examples of earlier costumes. The children could make on-site drawings of different fabric patterns and list the different types of fabric that were used at different periods in history.

Each child could copy a costume from a different period and then the class could make a costume time-line.

Follow-up
Set up a second fabric sorting exercise, but this time use a selection of fabric which would have been more commonly used in the past. The children can make a similar display of 'Materials used for clothes in the past'. Ask the children to consider other ways of sorting fabric, such as clothes worn by the very rich and the poor, clothes for hot and cold weather and so on.

Weaving loom

Age range
Eight to ten.

Group size
Pairs.

What you need
Per loom – four pieces of balsa wood about 15cm long and about 3cm thick, 20 one inch nails, ruler, pencil, hammer, thick wool.

What to do
Discuss with the children how many sorts of fabric are woven and how families in the past often wove their own cloth.

Ask the children to work in pairs to build their own looms. Tell them to put four pieces of balsa wood together to make a frame and nail them together at the corners. They should then use a ruler and pencil to mark two opposite ends of the frame at 1.5cm intervals. They should then hammer nails into these marks so that they go about halfway in to the wood. Tell them to tie wool to one of the corner nails and then to wind it across the frame around the first two nails on the opposite side. They should keep the wool taut at all times. Tell them to continue winding across the loom until they reach the last nail. They should then tie a knot and cut the wool. The loom is now ready for use.

The children should weave their own fabric using thick pieces of wool – the type used for rugs and tapestry. They should cut it into lengths about 10cm longer than the width of the loom and weave it under and over the frame, keeping it tightly pulled back until the piece is completed. Alternatively, they could use a card shuttle and a longer length of wool to help threading. A shuttle can be made by cutting a V shape at either end of a piece of strong card. Wool can then be wound around the shuttle. The shuttle is then passed over and under the warp threads so that the wefts are in place. The cloth is built up by passing the shuttle backwards and forwards across the loom from right to left and back again. When their cloth is finished they should cut the warp threads from the loom and fringe the ends.

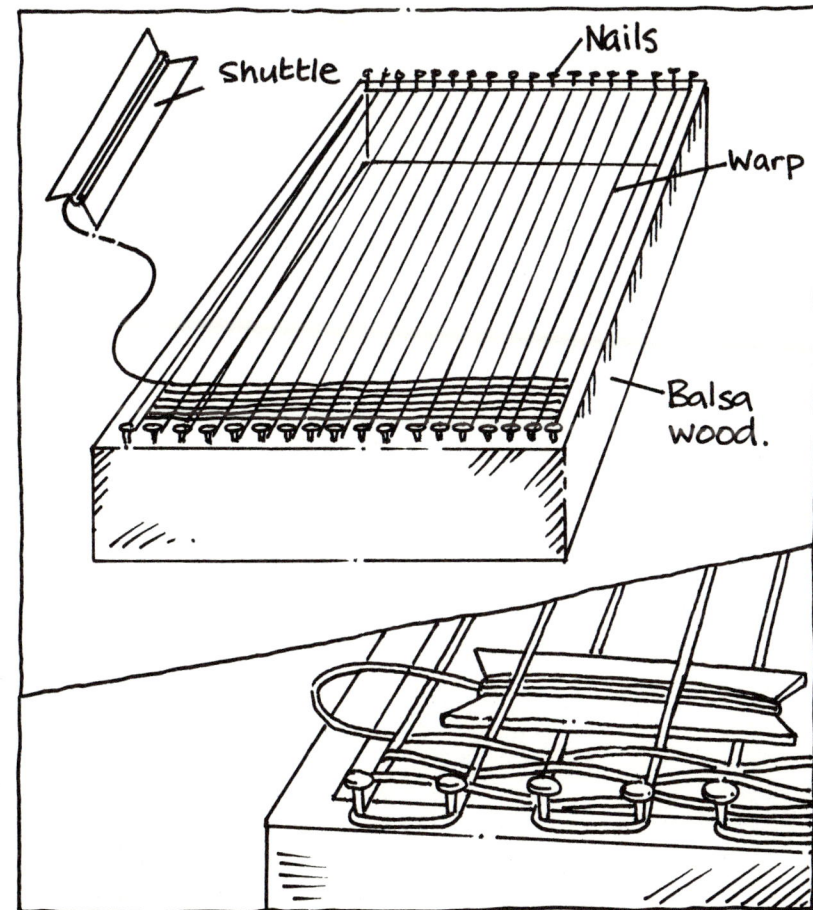

Building materials

Age range
Nine to eleven.

Group size
Small groups.

What you need
A collection of building materials such as brick, stone, wood, nails, tiles and so on; reference books about buildings, clay, leather off-cuts, twigs, scissors, joining materials (e.g. glue, adhesive tape, paste and so on).

What to do
Set up a display of different building materials and use it to encourage the children to investigate materials which were used for building homes in the past. The earliest type of home was a shelter in the rocks – usually a cave. Later tents were used by nomadic people who had to wander in search of food. These tents were made from animal skins and thin branches. Few tools were available so construction was simple.

Ask the children to research and make models of homes using clay, twigs and leather. Encourage them to construct the right setting for each type of house. For example, they could construct a rocky landscape out of clay and hollow out caves. They could embellish their models with trees and bushes. They could also make tent homes by making a twig framework and tying the ends together at the top. This should then be covered with a piece of leather. These models could be displayed on a forest or grassland site.

Follow-up
Let the children make other models of homes from the past using other materials. They can then display their models in chronological order. Ask them to investigate the effect bricks and brickmaking had on building and different types of roofing materials. Why were slate tiles so often used on Victorian houses?

History from non-history themes

Wool
- weaving;
- spinning:
- history of wool trde.

Wood
- wheels;
- carts;
- timber;
- paper.

Building
- metal;
- glass;
- brick;
- stone;
- wattle and daub;
- plaster.

Leather
- how made;
- Viking shoes;
- guilds.

Materials

Metals
- weapons;
- toys;
- coins;
- household objects.

Silk
- silk route:
  – Marco Polo;
- traders:
  – Venetians;
  – Portuguese;
  – Greek;
  – Spanish;
  – Roman.

Plastic
- household objects;
- furniture.

Clothes
- time line:
  – paintings;
  – portraits;
- fabrics used:
  – ribbons;
  – beads/jewels;
  – feathers.

Fur
- trade routes;
- companies e.g. Hudson Bay.

Communication

Nursery rhyme mime

Age range
Five to eight.

Group size
The whole class.

What you need
A nursery rhyme book.

What to do
Mime used to be a very popular form of entertainment. It was a very effective way of communicating with a wide variety of people from different areas and with different amounts of education. This form of play was often employed by strolling players such as the mummers.

   Use traditional nursery rhymes to teach the children basic miming skills. You should stress the importance of facial expression, body posture and gestures, underlining the need for bold clear movements. Practising such movements together will help children grasp the concept of mime. Remind the children that mime is *silent* acting and no words should be spoken! Ask one child to choose a rhyme and mime it to the rest of the class. The person who guesses what the rhyme is should then mime another rhyme to the class and so on. You may need to reread some of the rhymes to remind the children of ones they may have forgotten and you should keep the books handy so that they can get ideas for future sessions.

Follow-up
Ask the children to draw pictures of their favourite rhymes and also copy them out as handwriting practice. It will help them to remember rhymes for the next performance.

Postal frieze

Age range
Six to eight.

Group size
The whole class and small groups.

What you need
Writing materials, reference books on the postal service, board for a frieze, art materials.

What to do
Discuss with the children the process involved when communicating by letter. Talk about how letters were sent in the past and read the story of Rowland Hill and the invention of the Penny Post.

Ask each child to write a letter to the Head Office of the Postal Service asking for historical information about the postal service. Discuss how they should set out a letter and how they should address envelopes. Put each child's letter in its own envelope and then put them all in one big envelope.

Hopefully, you should receive sufficient information from these letters to make a frieze. Divide the frieze into various sections to show scenes of the postal system in chronological order, e.g, post rider, mail coach, mail train etc. Different groups can work on different sections. They should decide on the medium to be used for the frieze – paint, collage and so on.

Follow-up
Ask the children to write letters to other places which may be able to provide more information for the topic, for example a relevant book publishers. The children could post these letters individually, so that they receive individual letters in return. Organise a visit to a post office and/or sorting office if possible.

Stamp sorting

Age range
Six to eight.

Group size
Small groups.

What you need
Photocopiable pages 118 and 119, scissors, paste, one sheet of paper per child.

What to do
Give each child a sheet of paper, scissors and photocopiable page 118. They should cut out the stamps from the sheet and stick them on to their piece of paper in date order. When they have completed their sheets they can colour the stamps, using a Stanley Gibbons reference book or the actual stamps to find the correct colours. The children could go on to research the stories behind some of the stamps – the Royal Mail should be able to help. A collection of stamps can also prompt discussions about price increases over the years and important changes like decimalisation.

Follow-up
Ask the children to use photocopiable page 119 to design their own stamps. They might like to think of a design which commemorates a particular event. To give the children some ideas start by looking at a range of British commemorative stamps. The children could make their own collection of stamps which commemorate a particular event or person from the past.

Reading a picture

Age range
Six to nine.

Group size
Small groups.

What you need
A selection of old postcards showing people from the past, portraits and family groups, old photographs.

What to do
Lots of the information which we glean about the past is based upon our interpretation of visual images, such as photographs and paintings. Children need to be shown how to find out such information from such sources. This can be done by encouraging close observational skills as well as by encouraging them to ask questions.

Give the children some pictures and photographs to look at and a list of questions to answer. These questions should be concerned with the content of the picture:
• Who are the people in the picture?
• What is happening in the picture?
• When do you think the picture was taken?
• Where was the picture taken?
• What clues can you find to say whether the picture was posed or not?
• What do you think the people were feeling?

In pairs ask the children to look closely at a portrait and write down everything they 'know' about that person. They should then swap pictures with their partners and repeat the exercise without discussion. They can then compare their notes – do they both 'know' the same thing about the portrait?

Follow-up
Let the children choose one of the photographs and write a story about the person or people in it.

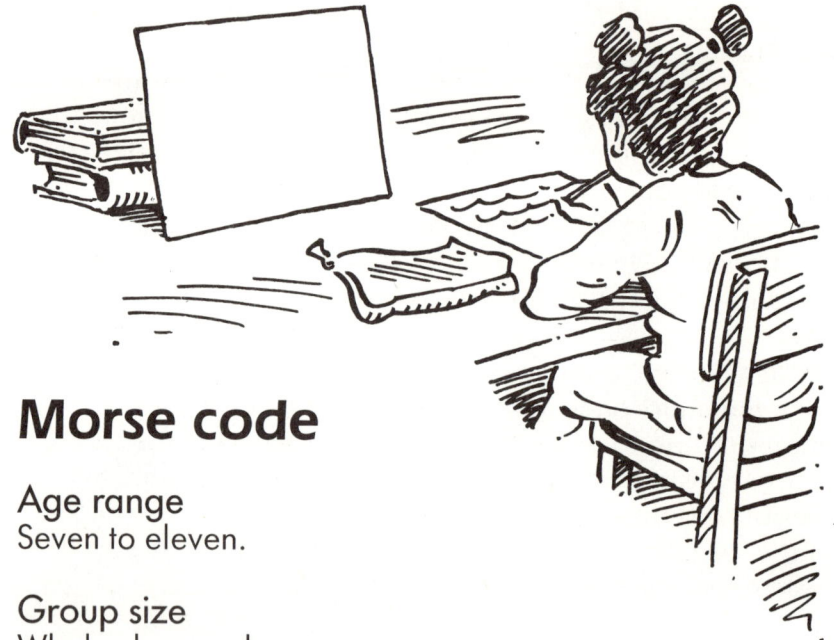

Morse code

Age range
Seven to eleven.

Group size
Whole class and groups.

What you need
Morse code sheet (photocopiable page 120), a selection of books about the use of Morse code, e.g., at sea, during the First World War and about the invention of telegraphic communication, torches.

What to do
Discuss as a whole class how Morse code was devised by Samuel Morse circa 1838. He devised a code in which letters are represented by combinations of long and short signals which can be written in dots and dashes. It can also be signalled with flash lamps or

radio bleeps. Telegraphic messages were easily transmitted by Morse code using a single wire machine, and this opened up a new method of communication.

Give each child photocopiable page 120 and let them write out a simple message using the code. They could then practise their message using light long and short taps.

In groups they should work out a message which could be communicated to another group using a torch to flash the coded message. This group would have to decode it and pass it on to the next group with an additional instruction.

The groups could then work on these messages so that they are able to dramatise a situation. For example, each group could act out a scene from a battlefront in the First World War. The scenes would be linked together by the need to transmit a message urgently.

Follow-up
Groups could look at the application of Morse code in 19th and 20th centuries. For example, how was Morse used in 1930s? In Edwardian times? In the 1960s?

This is one way of recording and communicating knowledge. Can the children devise others?

Inventions

Age range
Eight to eleven.

Group size
Small groups.

What you need
Reference books on communication, writing materials.

What to do
Discuss some of the more recent inventions that have enabled people to communicate more easily and quickly such as radio, cable, television, telephone, fax machines and so on. Talk about how these things came about through specific inventions. Divide the class into groups and set them a research task to find out about the history of some of these inventions and the people who invented them.

The information should be presented in 'comic strip' format. The children should divide their sheets of paper into six sections and relay, for exampe, the 'Story of the telephone' in six scenes with captions. They may prefer to do this individually.

Follow up
The children could make a class collection of old radios, telephones etc., so that they have an opportunity to examine the materials and designs used to make them.

History from non-history themes

Purpose
- need to change;
- effect on receiver;
- effect on sender;
- recording;
- influence:
  - propaganda.

Oral
- speech;
- songs;
- music:
  - folk
  - classical
  - popular
  - ways of recording
(CD/tape etc.)

Non-verbal
- mime;
- gesture/body language;
- sign language.

Technical innovations
- telephone;
- Morse code;
- cable;
- wireless;
- crystal set.

Communication

Written messages
- history of post:
  - P.O.
  - stamps
  - links with transport
- legends of sending messages:
  - 'How they brought the
Good News . . .';
  - Eros, Marathon.

Statistics
- shape;
- size;
- pattern;
- number;
- how used to assist
communication:
- computer language.

Visual image
- TV;
- fax;
- computer;
- advertising;
- display;
- types of written message,
postcards, birthday cards etc.

Printed word
- papers;
- books.

Distance
- where to?
- how long?

Pattern

Patchwork

Age range
Five to seven.

Group size
Small groups.

What you need
Display board, sugar paper, scissors, glue, pieces of fabric pre-cut into hexagon shapes, photocopiable page 121.

What to do
In the past fabric was scarce and expensive and therefore people would not even waste the scraps. Household furnishings often used material from old clothes, particularly dresses. The scraps were cut into various shapes and sewn together as patchwork. Quilts were one of the most popular things to make from patchwork.

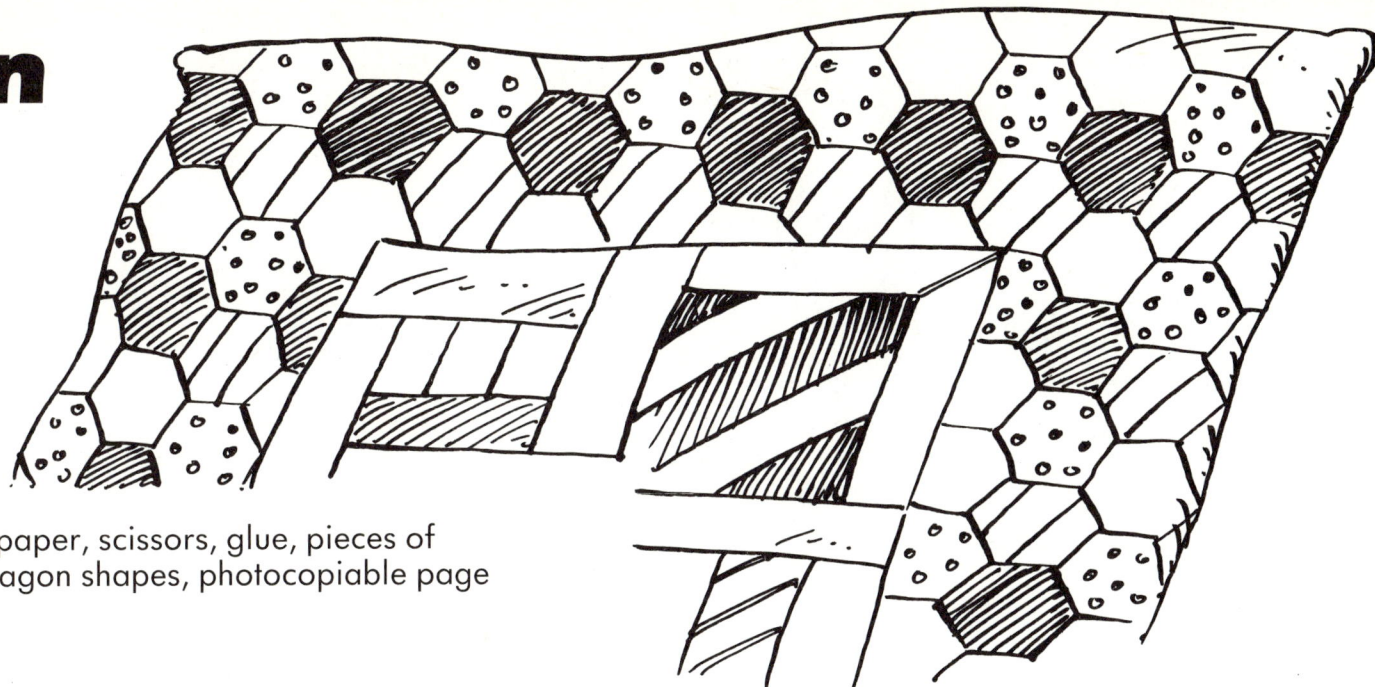

Make a frieze which features a row of beds; for example, this could be linked with 'Goldilocks and the Three Bears'. The children can then make some patchwork quilts for the beds. Ask them to cut a piece of sugar paper to the required quilt size. They should then cover the paper with fabric hexagons. They should select matching pieces of fabric in order to make patterns in the layout, and experiment with several versions before they glue them down. Make sure that the pieces all tessellate.

Follow-up
Give the children a set of either paper or fabric hexagons and ask them to see how many symmetrical patterns they can make. They should record their successes by drawing the patterns into the pre-drawn sheet on photocopiable page 121.

81

When the children have completed this sheet they can tackle a more difficult version. This time they will need to cut out pieces of coloured self-adhesive paper to the same size as the shapes on the sheet and fill in the pattern. They can use their coloured sheets as a colour guide.

Follow-up
Once the children have become familiar with this type of design and can work with accuracy on symmetrical patterns they could design their own pattern sheets.

The coloured paper sheets could be laminated and then cut up to form quite a complex jigsaw.

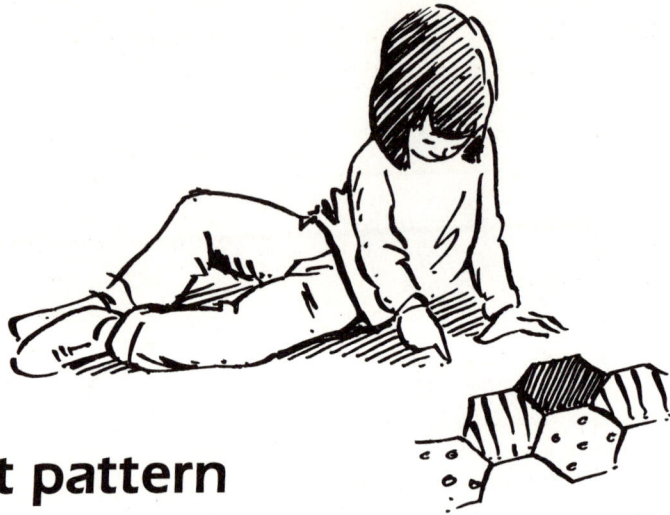

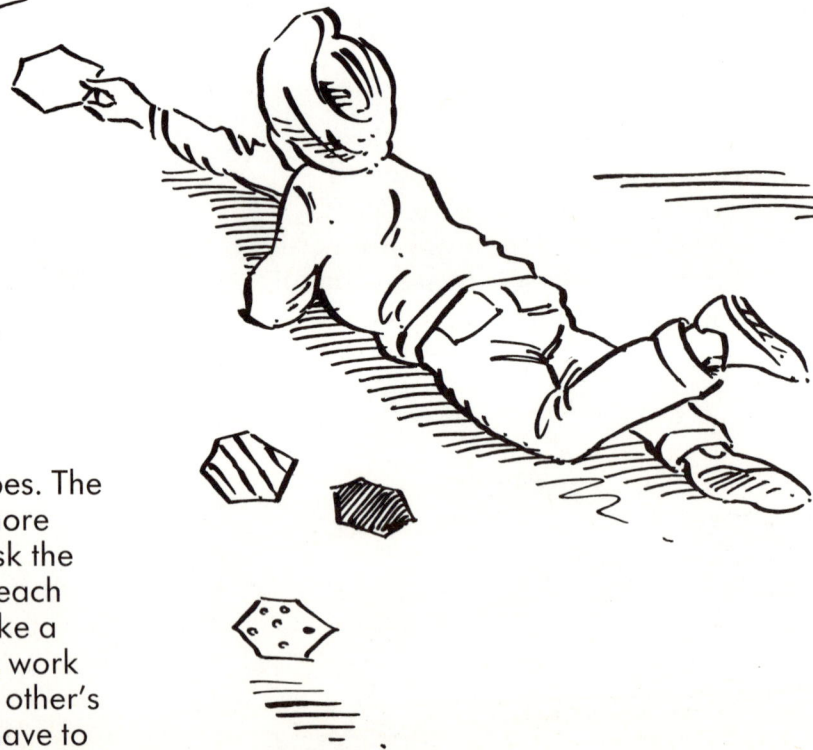

Quilt pattern

Age range
Seven to nine.

Group size
Pairs.

What you need
Coloured self-adhesive paper, colouring pens or pencils, scissors, photocopiable page 122.

What to do
Patchwork was often made with a variety of shapes. The 'quilt' sheet on photocopiable page 122 uses a more complicated design than the simple hexagons. Ask the children to work together to make sure that they each colour the pattern symmetrically. Tell them to make a fold down the centre of the sheet so that they can work on half each, making sure that they 'mirror' each other's colours. This will mean, of course, that they will have to discuss and agree on the colours to be used!

HOME SWEET HOME

Cross-stitch names

Age range
Seven to nine.

Group size
Small groups.

What you need
Small pieces of binca, needles, coloured thread, pencils, small pieces of squared paper.

What to do
Tapestry and needlepoint have been popular throughout history. Show the children pictures of the Bayeau Tapestry. In the Medieval period tapestries were used to adorn the bare walls of castles, and the women of the household made needlepoint cushions and covers. In Victorian times many children learned needlework skills by making samplers. Sometimes they made them just using cross-stitch – letters, numbers, flowers and abstract patterns were popular subject matter. Children often wrote their own names and a motto such as 'Early to bed, early to rise, makes a man healthy, wealthy and wise.'

Tell the children that they are going to make their own samplers. They should start with their initials and then they can move on to embroider their full names. Tell them to use the squared paper and mark out their initials with crosses on the squares. They should then copy this on to the binca, marking the same number of squares. They should then stitch the design using cross-stitch.

Follow-up
When the children feel confident with cross-stitch they can complete their names. They could also have a go at sewing a very simple sampler consisting of a motto with a border edging.

Banners

Age range
Nine to eleven.

Group size
Small groups.

What you need
Sheets of A6 paper, pencils, paints, string, reference books showing flags, shields and banners.

What to do
Discuss with the children how flags and shields were used as a means of identifying people in battle. Since soldiers were covered in armour from head to toe they needed 'colours' to show whose side they were on. Look at some of the designs together and discuss which colours and emblems were popular.

Ask the children to work in groups and think of a design for a banner. Explain that the banner should show symbols rather than illustrations, e.g. bars, chevrons, the fleur-de-lis and so on, and that the predominant colours used in the past were gold, azure, red, black and white. They should sketch their designs in pencil on rough paper first and then fill a sheet of A6 with their designs. When completed the banners can be hung in the 'baronial classroom'.

Follow-up
The children could use the same designs to make shields. They could investigate designs for family crests and mottoes and try to create one for their own family. They could look further at the devices and colours used in heraldry and make a chart of them.

Printing block

Age range
Seven to nine.

Group size
Groups of four.

What you need
Paper, pencils, reference books showing textile patterns; pieces of patterned fabric, books showing clear pictures of flowers; potatoes, knives or pressprint, paint.

What to do
Traditionally, many textile and fabric designs used nature as the source of inspiration with designs being based on stylised forms of leaves and flowers. Ask the children to create their own printing blocks based on a flower or leaf.

First encourage the children to spend some time looking through the books and pieces of fabric and to discuss the patterns they find and how they are printed. Tell them to choose a particular flower or leaf to use for their blocks. Suggest that they choose a fairly simple one with a bold shape and not too many overlapping petals, for example a tulip or a pansy. They should practise drawing their designs on paper before they copy them on to the pressprint. If the children are making potato prints they will need to cut the design into the top of the potato, so the design must be really simple. Potato blocks will not last and therefore won't be much use after the end of the session. They are, however, easy to acquire and satisfying to use. Let the children decide which type of block they will make.

The completed blocks can be used to print wallpaper, wrapping paper or book covers. The blocks could also be used with fabric inks/paints and printed on fabric.

Follow up
The fabric which has been printed with blocks could be used to make simple costumes or provide a background display on Pattern.

Local pattern hunt

Age range
Nine to eleven.

Group size
Small groups.

What you need
Reference books on buildings in the past and architecture, clipboards, pencils, paper, camera (optional).

What to do
Talk as a class about where patterns can be found in architecture. Ask the children to work on different aspects such as windows, doors, brick patterns, iron work, tiles and so on. From their research they should compile a reference sheet of designs to look for which they should then share with the rest of the class.

Organise the children into groups and take them on a local pattern hunt. They should take their reference sheets and clipboards with them. Encourage the children to look particularly for 'old' buildings and for a variety of types of building. They should tick off their reference sheets as they find specific examples of patterns, and also record new ones by drawing and photographing them. Again, each group can look for different aspects.

Once back in the classroom each group can make a book of their findings, for example, 'Local brick patterns', using drawings, photographs and some information about each pattern. Ask them to try and date the examples of older and newer bonds.

Follow up
Use a database to record the most common pattern found. How many were angular? How many were circular?

History from non-history themes

Clothes
- fabrics;
- textiles.

Interior design
- tiles;
- wallpaper;
- decoration, e.g. stencils

Design
- William Morris;
- Paisley;
- Celtic design;
- Willow pattern;
- tartan;
- mosaics.

Moulds
   – plaster moulds;
   – jelly moulds.
- foundry;

Pattern

Furniture
- china/cutlery:
   – gilding.
   – engraving.

Environment
- wrought iron;
- doors/windows;
- bricks/tiles;
- stained glass.

Pattern in painting
- abstract;
- lives of artists.

Garden design
- formal gardens of past:
   – Knot gardens
   – Pitmedden.

Graphic design
- writing patterns.

Printing techniques
- history of;
- technological developments.

Light and colour

Cave paintings

Age range
Five to seven.

Group size
Groups of four.

What you need
Paper, powder paints, water, twigs, feathers, straws, pictures of cave paintings.

What to do
Let the children look at a selection of pictures of cave paintings and discuss with them how these pictures usually show wild animals and hunters. Discuss the colours used in the paintings and the painting materials that were available to the cave dwellers. Twigs, reeds and feathers were used instead of brushes and coloured rocks were crushed to produce pigments which were then mixed with fat.

Ask the children to simulate cave painting by using twigs, feathers and straws instead of brushes. They should use a few powder paint colours – try to use 'earth' tones which can be mixed from brown, green, black, white, blue plus a little red and yellow. Tell the children to experiment first before they begin to paint by mixing very small quantities of dry powder paint and pretending that it is finely ground rock dust. When they have produced a muted mix such as yellow ochre, they can add a little water and paint a cave picture.

Follow up
Create a larger version of a cave painting which can be worked on by a group of six. This can then be displayed on the wall of your classroom 'cave'.

Discuss how many paints and dyes today are still made from natural materials.

Vegetable dyes

Age range
Five to seven.

Group size
Groups of four.

What you need
Small pieces of red cabbage, beetroot, carrot, a few pea-pods, onion skins and blackberries; old saucepan, strainer, knife, potato masher, pudding bowls, mug, water, alum fixer (or Dylon cold-water fix), access to stove, small pieces of white cotton (old sheeting), old newspapers, gloves.

What to do
Talk with the children about the way fabrics were dyed in the past – using natural plant and vegetable dyes. Many of these colourings are still used today, such as heather and bracken in Scottish woollen cloth. Let the children examine the selection of vegetables and fruits which will provide dyes. They will not be surprised by the blackberries, since their stain is obvious, but they may not expect onion skins to produce any colour.

Throughout this activity encourage the children to hypothesise and predict what might happen.

Try making one vegetable dye at a time. You will need to give the children a lot of support in this as safety is paramount. Cover the table with newspaper and chop up one of the vegetables as finely as possible and then crush it carefully. Soak it for about five minutes in two mugfuls of water and then boil it in this water for 20 minutes. Check that it doesn't boil away! When it is cool, strain the liquid off into a pudding bowl. Soak the fabric in a solution of alum fixer and water for a few minutes. Take it out and add it to the dye in the saucepan and simmer it for 15 minutes. Remove the material and place it on a wad of newspaper to dry.

Follow up
Repeat the process with a variety of other vegetables and fruit. You can then mount the dyed fabric samples on to a wall chart. Ask the children to write out a step-by-step guide to the dyeing process in chart form using as many pictures as possible. Dye a larger piece of material for use in displays. The children could experiment with different quantities of vegetables and water to see if this affects the shades of colour produced.

Candles

Age range
Five to seven.

Group size
The whole class and small groups.

What you need
A large collection of candles of different shapes, sizes and colours; paper, water paint.

What to do
Discuss with the class how candles used to be the main indoor light source. They were made every autumn by each household in their hundreds so that there would be a big enough supply to last the whole winter. Talk about the variety of candle shapes and colour in your collection. Most candles in the past were a functional white, though they were made in a variety of sizes. Ask the children to bring in candles and set up a candle shop. In small groups the children can pretend to buy and sell the candles in the shop. This role-playing activity encourages children to consider the use of candles in the past and appreciate their importance as a main light source before the invention of electricity. It will also help them to understand what it was like to live in the past without electricity.

Also let the children make candle resist paintings. Give each child a sheet of paper and a candle and tell them to draw a picture on it with the candle, making sure that they make a fairly thick mark so that plenty of wax sticks to the paper. They should then paint over the picture with a wash of watered down paint. The paint will not stay on the waxed picture. This will help young children to understand something of the properties of candles. They should understand the reasons for using candlewax for light rather than say, clay or metal. They can also consider the purpose of the wick and the ease with which it is possible to include it into the wax. The children should gain an empathy for the past through the shop role play which will give an insight into how candles were made, used, bought and sold.

Follow-up
Ask the children to find out how candles were made in the past and possibly have a go at candle making. They can use a variety of containers as candle moulds. However, this is an activity that requires careful adult supervision because of the hot temperature needed to melt the wax.

Stencilling

Age range
Seven to nine.

Group size
Small groups.

What you need
Photocopiable page 123, scissors, paste, pieces of card (old cereal boxes will do), brushes, paints, paper in a selection of colours.

What to do
In the days before wallpaper, stencilling was a common technique used to decorate the inside of houses. Many ceilings, walls and pieces of furniture in Tudor and

Stuart times, for example, were decorated in this way. It was a fairly simple way of creating an attractive design and could be used in a variety of patterns and colours.

Ask the children to work in groups to produce different colour variations, e.g, red and pink, blue and green, using the stencil provided on photocopiable page 123. They will need to cut out the shaded areas on the sheet and then mount it on to a sheet of card. They should then place the card stencil over a sheet of paper and paint over the top of it. Tell the children to lift the stencil off the sheet carefully and leave the painting to dry. The children can try using a variety of paint and paper colours. The stencils themselves can be completed using one or more colours at each go.

Follow-up
Try particular colour ways – such as shades of green, or blues and purples, white paint only on black paper, rose pink on red paper and so on. The completed stencilled work can be used as a border around a display, or used to decorate the play area.

Candle-light

Age range
Seven to nine.

Group size
The whole class.

What you need
Plain white candles, candlesticks with firm bases, dark room, books, paper, pens.

What to do
Talk with the children about what it must have been like living before gas and electric lighting illuminated our homes. Discuss how any work such as reading, writing letters and sewing that needed to be done after dark had to be completed by candle-light. How would it have felt? Would it have been easy to read for long periods by candle-light? Would this hurt their eyes?

Set up an experiment for children to experience working by candle-light. Make the classroom as dark as possible so that the candle-light will show up. It is best to do this on a dark winter afternoon. Sit in a circle on a carpeted area with the candlesticks in the middle of the circle. Light the candles and give each child a book to read for about ten minutes. (This is too short a time to harm their eyes, but make sure that anyone who has sight impairment is in a good light.)

After ten minutes turn the lights on and discuss what it was like to read by candle-light, and try to encourage imaginative descriptions.

Give each child a piece of paper and ask them to write about the experience. They could do this in the form of a letter to a friend, for example 'Dear . . . I am writing to you by candle-light . . .'.

Follow-up
Ask the children to find out about how candles were used in the past and customs associated with them. What, for instance, is the origin of Candlemas Day?

Davy lamp

Age range
Nine to eleven.

Group size
Pairs.

What you need
Photocopiable page 124, writing materials, reference books on mining.

What to do
Ask the children to read the extract about mine conditions and discuss the problems of safety. How do they think they would have felt working in a coal mine at

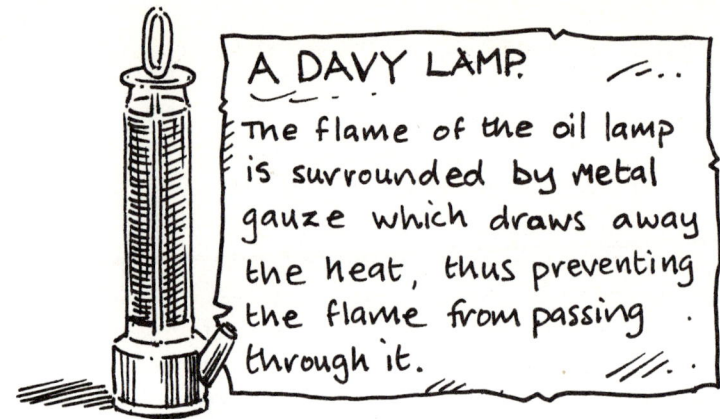

A DAVY LAMP.
The flame of the oil lamp is surrounded by metal gauze which draws away the heat, thus preventing the flame from passing through it.

that time? Ask them to write a short piece imagining that they were miners before the invention of the Davy lamp. When they have done this they should find out as much as they can about the invention of the Davy lamp. What led to its development? How was it made? Where was it first used? Was it used in all mines? How long did it take before it was universally used? Was any legislation needed to enforce its use? Was there any opposition to it? Was there a lessening of the number of accidents as a result? Who was Sir Humphrey Davy?

Much of this information may be found in the reference books which you have provided, but further research may also be needed. What will the children need to do to get this information and verify their findings with primary source material? Ask them to list the possible source materials that they will need for this.

Working in pairs the children shoudl follow-up some of these ideas by looking at newspapers from the period, mining records, contemporary drawings and written accounts such as diaries. They may need to write to libraries and archives for examples of this sort of material. When their research is complete they should present their findings in a written account to the rest of the class.

History from non-history themes

Vegetable and plant dyes
- their effect on art.
- how alum was obtained;
- dye industry;
- paints and pigments;

Decoration
- cave painting;
- famous artists;
- decorative techniques;
- printing.

Photography
- films;
- TV;
- introduction of colour.

Battle colours
- flags;
- banners;
- shields;
- chivalry.

Optical inventions
- telescope;
- binoculars;
- glasses.

Light and colour

Colours in old fabrics
- popular colours for clothes;
  - women
  - men e.g. grey suits
- old paintings showing use
of gold and silver in clothes:
  - field of the 'cloth of gold'.

Lighting
- homes;
- streets;
- mines:
  - Humphrey Davy.

Oil
- early inventions.

How light travels
- experiments;
- inventions.

Electric
- Edison.

Candles
- when first used;
- developments from candles;
- life before electricity.

Gas
- discovery of;
- early use in the home.

Time

Easter biscuits

Age range
Five to seven.

Group size
Small groups (not more than six in each group).

What you need
200g flour, 100g butter, 100g sugar, a handful of currants, ½ teaspoon mixed spice and cinnamon, squeeze of lemon, beaten egg, rolling pin, board, round cutters, baking tray, access to oven.

What to do
Discuss with the children how lots of events are commemorated by making and eating traditional food and how particular dishes are eaten to mark various celebrations and festivals. One such time is the Christian festival of Easter when Easter biscuits are traditionally eaten.

The children can make the biscuits by rubbing the butter and flour together and then stirring in the sugar, currants, spices and lemon. They should then mix in the egg to form a dough. The dough should be placed on a floured board and rolled out thinly. They should then use the cutters to cut the mixture into 5cm rounds. Place the biscuits on to a greased baking tray and cook them on gas mark 5/6 or 190°/200°C for 10 minutes. The children could then package the biscuits attractively for Easter gifts.

Follow-up
Discuss other foods that are traditionally eaten at various celebrations. Ask the children to make a list of them in a calendar format and find and write out some of their recipes. You can then set up further cooking sessions.

Period houses

Age range
Five to seven.

Group size
Small groups.

What you need
Photocopiable page 125, scissors, paste, colouring pencils, sheets of card, LEGO figures.

What to do
Over the past thousand years there have been many different styles of houses. All these are associated with different historical periods. Ask the children to look at the styles shown on photocopiable page 125. The earlier styles were mainly built from timber. The children should colour in the sheet, then stick it to a sheet of card and cut out the houses. Glue a small strip of card to the back so that they stand up. The houses can be used for small-world play using LEGO figures. This activity will foster discussion on house styles and building methods and develop observational skills and historical knowledge.

Follow-up
The houses can be arranged in a time-line. Go on to read and talk about stories which relate to a particular style or period, for example, The Great Fire of London. LEGO could be also used to recreate historical scenes.

Commemorative plate design

Age range
Seven to nine.

Group size
Small groups.

What you need
Books about particular important historical events, examples of commemorative plates, card, pencils, water colour paints, fine brushes.

What to do
Show the children examples of commemorative plates and discuss with them how important events such as royal weddings and coronations are commemorated in this way. In the past jugs and plates were also often decorated to commemorate more personal events, such as family Christenings.

Read to the children a number of accounts of famous historical events – four will probably be enough. If possible choose some that they may already be familiar with such as Guy Fawkes and the Gunpowder Plot, the Battle of Hastings, Florence Nightingale and the Crimean War, the invention of the railway or the Great Fire of London. Discuss some of the key elements of each story so that the children can begin to think about the images they will use.

Ask each group to choose a different story and let them work together looking through the relevant reference books for illustration ideas. They should practise different design ideas on rough paper until they have decided on one. Give each child a plate-sized circular piece of card and ask them to draw, in pencil, the outline of the design. Finally, they should colour in their design with water colour paints and do the lettering in paint or felt-tipped pen.

Follow-up
Ask the children to make further plates to commemorate other stories. They could also think about other events which they could make plates for. Some of the simplest designs could be transferred to clay plates.

Festival calendar

Age range
Seven to nine.

Group size
Small groups.

What you need
Large piece of paper for a wall chart, reference books on festivals, paper, writing materials, felt-tipped pens.

What to do
Talk with the children about the traditional nature of festivals and customs. Most festivals have been celebrated for hundreds of years with some customs being adapted to meet changing beliefs. For example, many Pagan customs have been adapted to Christian needs. Divide up a large sheet of paper into 12 sections, one section to represent each month. Ask the children to list as many festivals and customs as they can, including festivals from as many different religions and cultures as possible.

Divide the class into groups to research the origins of particular festivals. They should then write up and illustrate their findings. Each piece of work can then be mounted on the large sheet of paper under the correct month.

Follow-up
Ask the children to work on one particular festival so that it can be presented at an assembly. They can make traditional artefacts and dramatise some of its associated customs. Do many religions share the same time of year for celebration, for example December and April?

Famous people time-line

Age range
Nine to eleven.

Group size
Small groups.

What you need
A very large collection of history books, paper, pens.

What to do
Make a time-line that goes all around the classroom.
Divide the time-line up into centuries and then subdivide
it by decades. Fix this at a height which is easily
accessible and readable for the children.

Ask the children to find as many famous people as
they can and write their names across the correct
decades on the time-line to indicate their life spans.
They will need to work in groups to research these
dates.

This activity could take place over a number of
sessions and will take time to complete. Once the names
are all correctly filled in, the children can illustrate the
line by drawing pictures of some of these famous
people.

One of the main reasons for doing the activity is not
just to learn something about chronology, but also to
look at the way history is represented by historians of a
later date. Once the line is complete you will be able to
see that a particular set of people are on your line. Why
were they regarded as famous? Do the children think
they deserve to be? Why is there little mention in the
books about ordinary men and women? Why are so few
women famous? What makes a person famous?

Follow-up
The children can research some of the individuals shown
on the time-line further, building up a pocket *This was
your life* dossier on their favourite characters.

As a class, you can discuss who of today's figures is
likely to be regarded as famous in the future. How can
we ensure that the lives of ordinary men and women are
recorded so that their history is not forgotten?

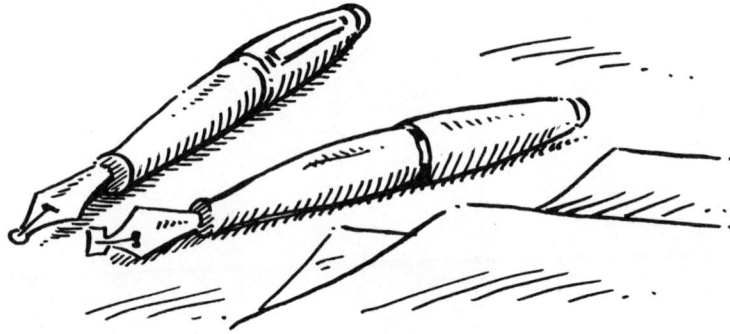

Time rhyme book

Age range
Nine to eleven.

Group size
Small groups.

What you need
A collection of nursery rhyme books, song books and poems (avoid those written very recently); calligraphy pens, plain white paper, a home-made class book.

What to do
Read to the class a few of the songs and rhymes from the nursery rhyme books which deal with time, for example 'Hickory, dickory dock'. (There are many rhymes that refer to the seasons.) Ask the children to think of any more rhymes that they know and make a note of them. Explain that many of these rhymes are very old and refer to ways of life and incidents from centuries ago. Ask the children to look through the books to find as many 'time' rhymes and poems as they can. They should make a list of all the titles and share their findings with the rest of the class.

Depending on how many have been found, the children can copy them out on to white paper using the calligraphy pens. They will obviously have to use their best handwriting. The completed rhymes should be carefully pasted into the class book and each child can read their own choice to the class.

Follow-up
Ask pairs of children to take a particular nursery rhyme and research its origin. The resulting information can be mounted in a zigzag book with illustrations to accompany the time rhyme book. These can then be shared with younger children in the school.

History from non-history themes

Ways of measuring and recording time
- clocks:
  - watches
  - digital
  - GMT
- sun dials;
- shadows;
- water clock;
- candle clock.

Calendars
- Julian;
- Roman;
- Arabic;
- days of the week:
  - Norse legends
  - hours and minutes.

Periods of time
- Egyptian;
- Roman;
- Stuart;
- how named/dated.

People in the past
- life stories;
- diaries.

Time

Festivals
- special times.

Houses in the past
- changes through different periods.

Commemorating events
- anniversaries and holidays.

Stories about time
- poems (e.g. Elizabethan sonnets);
- survey of monuments;
- life expectancy/life span.

Musical development
- songs;
- nursery rhymes.

Reproducible material

Recording sheet, see page 7

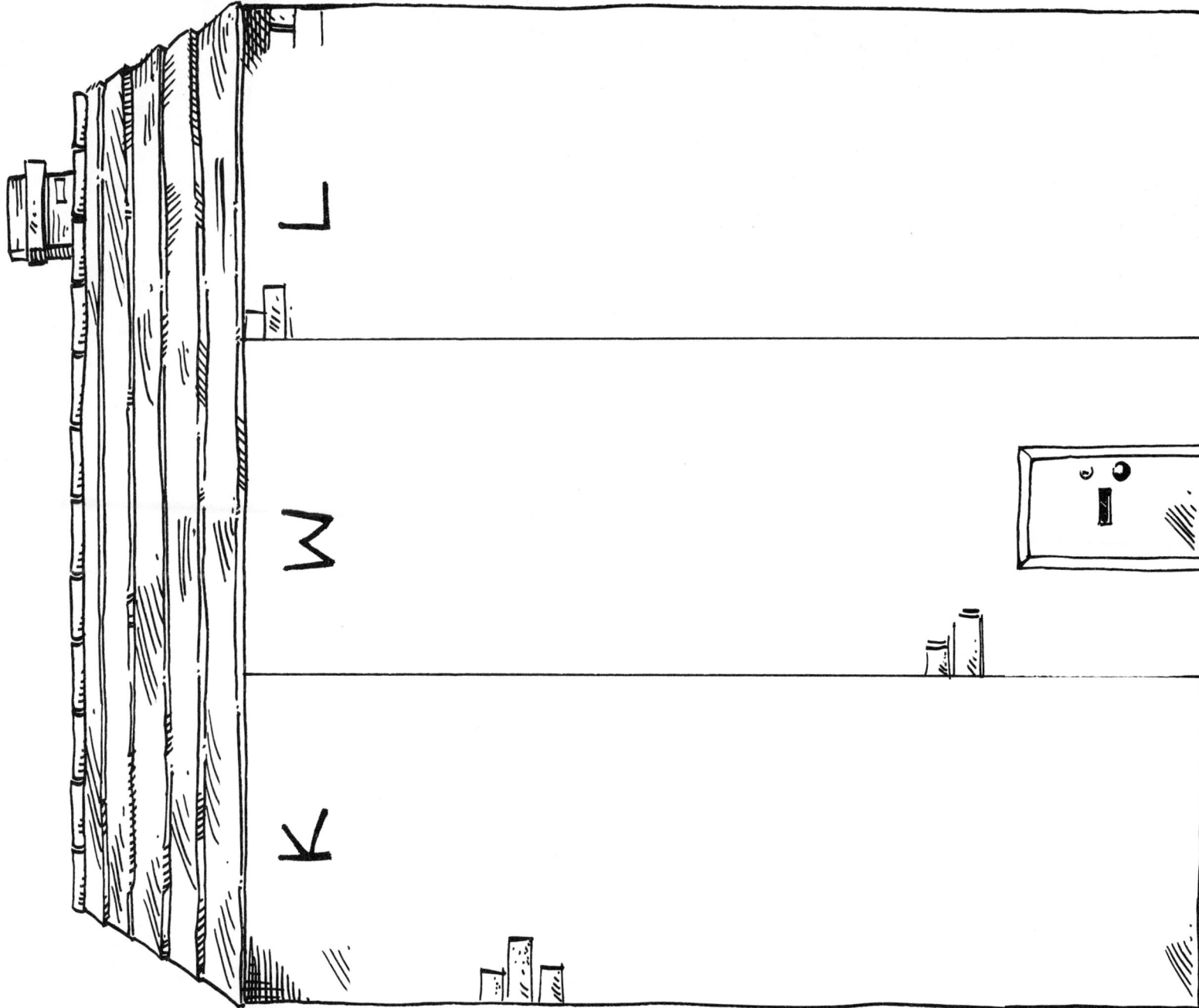

K – What I KNOW about
W – WHAT I want to find out about
L – What I LEARNED about

L

W

K

Vocabulary chart, see page 9

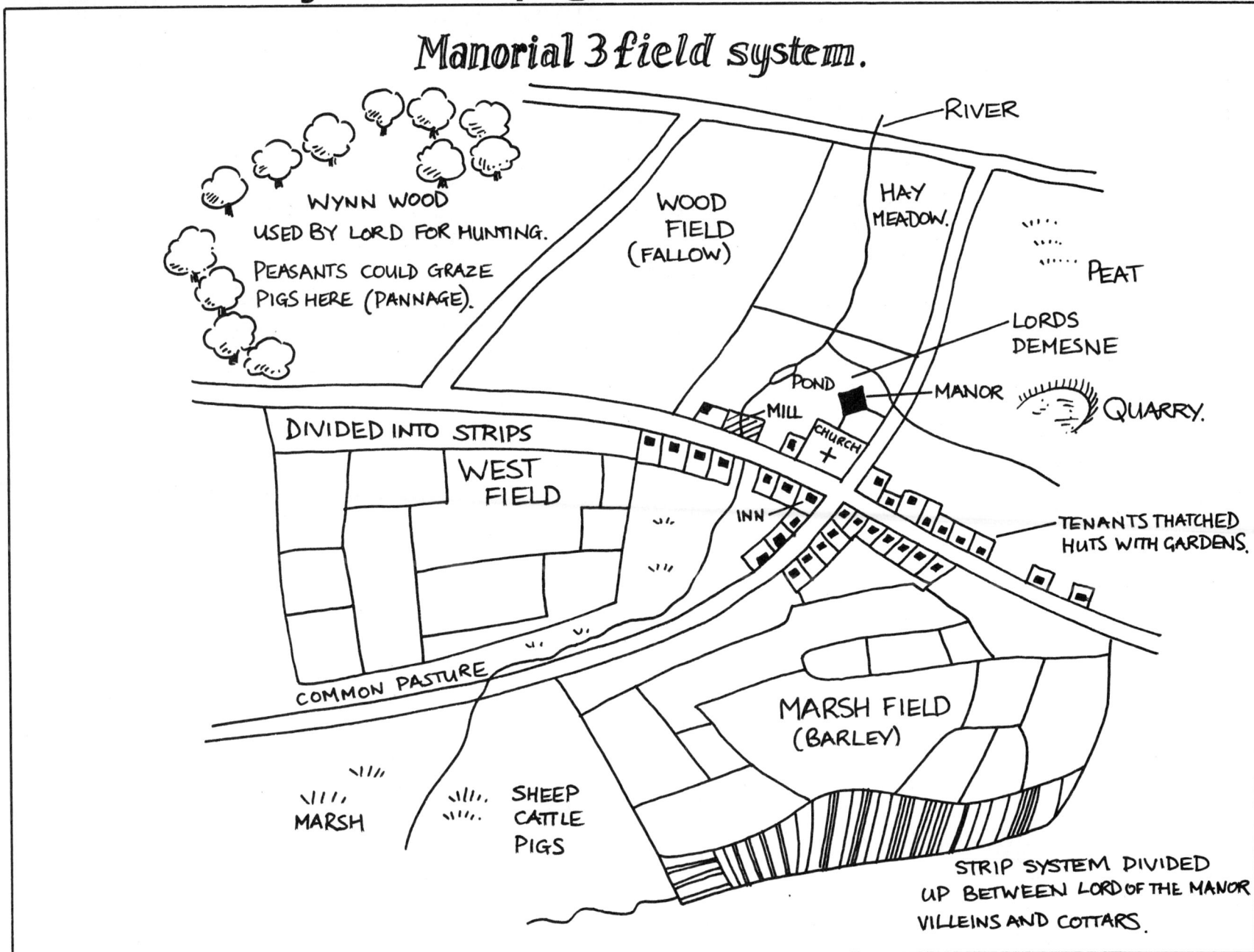

Manorial 3 field system.

RIVER

WYNN WOOD
USED BY LORD FOR HUNTING.
PEASANTS COULD GRAZE PIGS HERE (PANNAGE).

WOOD FIELD (FALLOW)

HAY MEADOW.

PEAT

LORDS DEMESNE

POND

MILL

MANOR

QUARRY.

CHURCH +

DIVIDED INTO STRIPS

WEST FIELD

INN

TENANTS THATCHED HUTS WITH GARDENS.

COMMON PASTURE

MARSH FIELD (BARLEY)

MARSH

SHEEP CATTLE PIGS

STRIP SYSTEM DIVIDED UP BETWEEN LORD OF THE MANOR VILLEINS AND COTTARS.

Old and new kitchens, see page 25

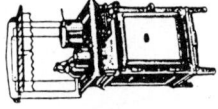

This page may be photocopied for use in the classroom and should not be declared in any return in respect of any photocopying licence.

Give *Pleasure*

Give *Health*

Give *an 'Instant'*

🌲 *The Gift that keeps on giving!*

Day in, day out, an "Instant" gives a ready supply of delicious, clear fruit juice at a stroke of the lever. It's the **permanent gift**—strong, beautifully finished, polished aluminium. Of ironmongers and stores.

As illustrated, 20/-.
"Instant" No. 2, 12/6.

"INSTANT" JUICE PRESS

NORUP LTD., 78. Fore St., London, E.C.2

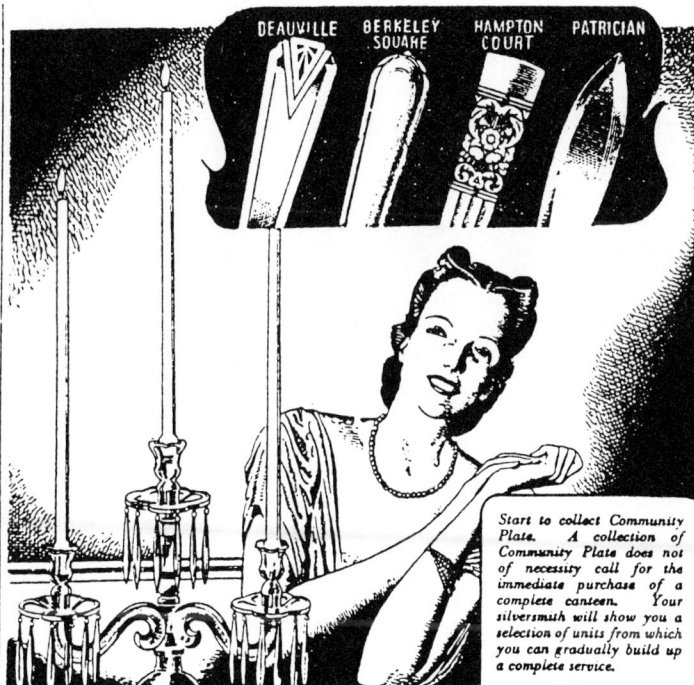

DEAUVILLE · BERKELEY SQUARE · HAMPTON COURT · PATRICIAN

The glow of candle light ... and every subtle flicker reflects the infinite beauty of Community Plate. Guest upon guest will envy the grace of your perfectly proportioned plate, whilst you yourself will ponder as the years pass on the lasting, enduring beauty of true Sheffield craftsmanship.

Start to collect Community Plate. A collection of Community Plate does not of necessity call for the immediate purchase of a complete canteen. Your silversmith will show you a selection of units from which you can gradually build up a complete service.

Free!

TABLE KNOWLEDGE
by Joan Woollcombe

Written by an eminent authority this invaluable booklet clearly explains how to set the table on all occasions. It also deals with the care of silverware. Free copy on application to Community, 264(F) Regent Street, W.1.

COMMUNITY PLATE
At all Leading Silversmiths

also TUDOR PLATE — unusual values at lower prices

★ *Insist on*

A.G
BRAND ELVAS PLUMS

PERFECT COFFEE

quickly and easily made by using **DAVY'S PERFECTION COFFEE** with

DAVY'S 'PULVO' COFFEE FILTER

In return for P.O. 5/- we will send one Filter as illustrated (jug not included) and one lb. of Coffee.

Satisfaction is guaranteed and repeat orders for this delightful Coffee (in air-tight tins, 2/8 per lb. postage paid) are sure to follow.

A. DAVY & SONS LTD
COFFEE SPECIALISTS FOR OVER 40 YEARS
38 & 40 Fargate, SHEFFIELD.

EAT **NUTTALL'S MINTOES** AFTER MEALS
PER QR 4d · 4d

Old and new kitchens, see page 25

A Victorian kitchen

The Viking alphabet

The Viking alphabet was called the futhork.
The letters were known as runes.

ᛏ B ᛒ ᚴ ᛁ ᛁ ᚠ ᚠ ᛪ ᚼ ᛁ ᚱ ᚱᛏ ᛙ ᛏ ᛕ ᚴ ᚱ ᛖ ᚿ ᛁ ᛨ ᛪ ᛪᛪ

a b c d e f g h ij K l m n o p q r s t uvw x y z

Colour in and cut out.

Rune stones.

Can you read what they say?

The ancient Egyptians used pictures as letters.
They called these hieroglyphs.

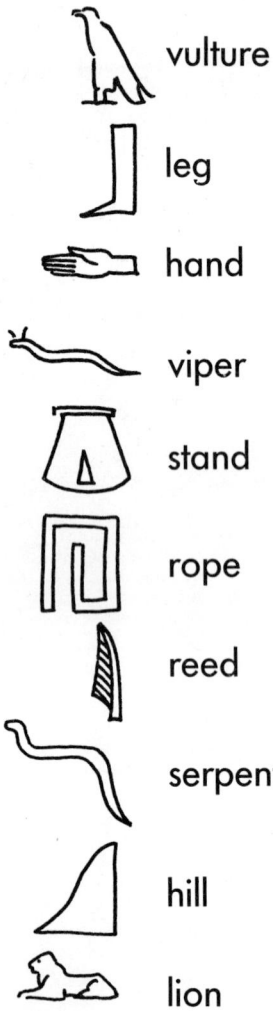

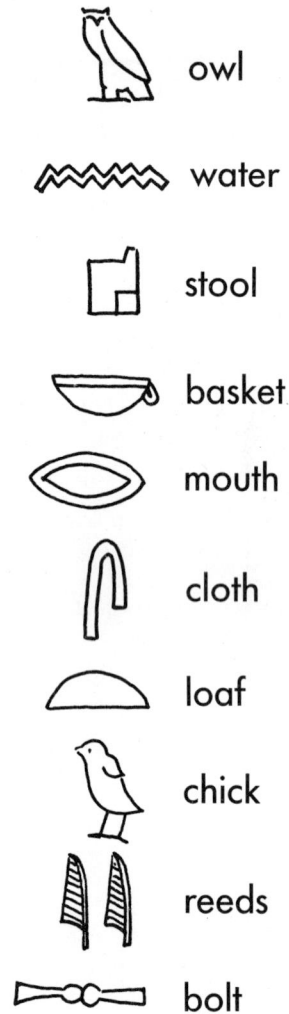

vulture	owl
leg	water
hand	stool
viper	basket
stand	mouth
rope	cloth
reed	loaf
serpent	chick
hill	reeds
lion	bolt

Ancient Egyptian

Britain's railway network in 1844

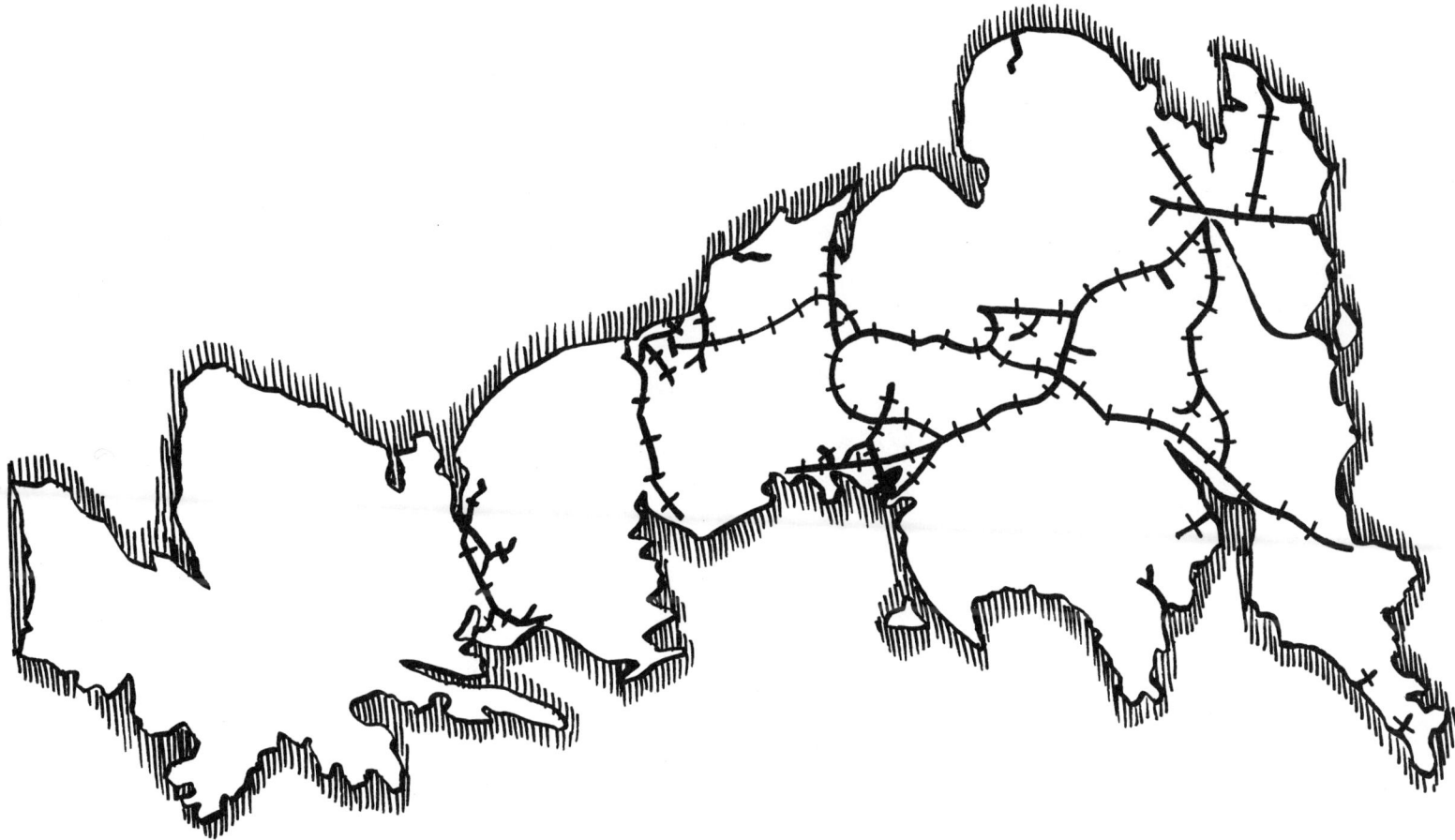

Railway drama, see page 36

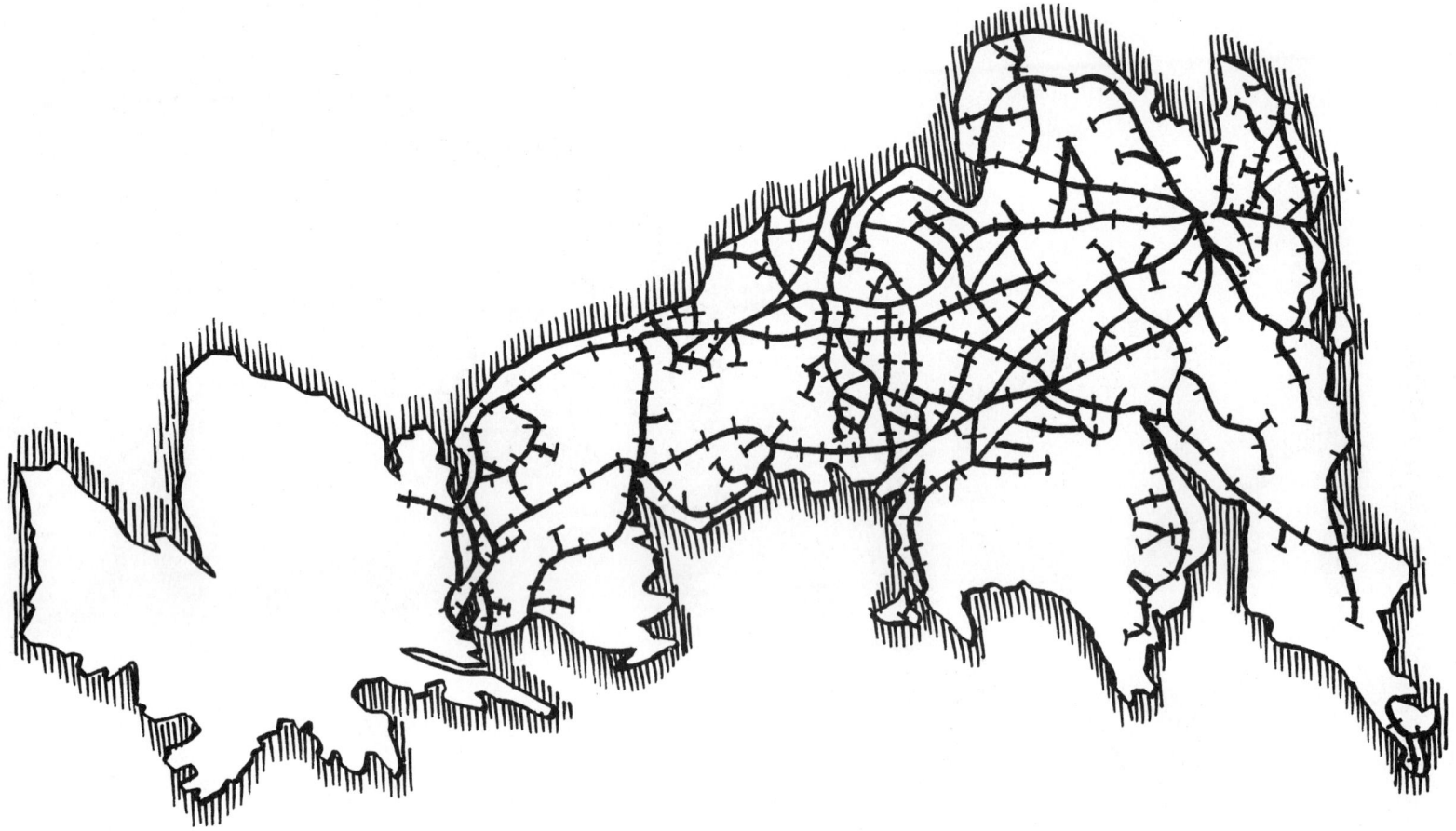

Britain's railway network in 1852

Railway drama, see page 36

Britain's railway network in 1914

Railway drama, see page 36

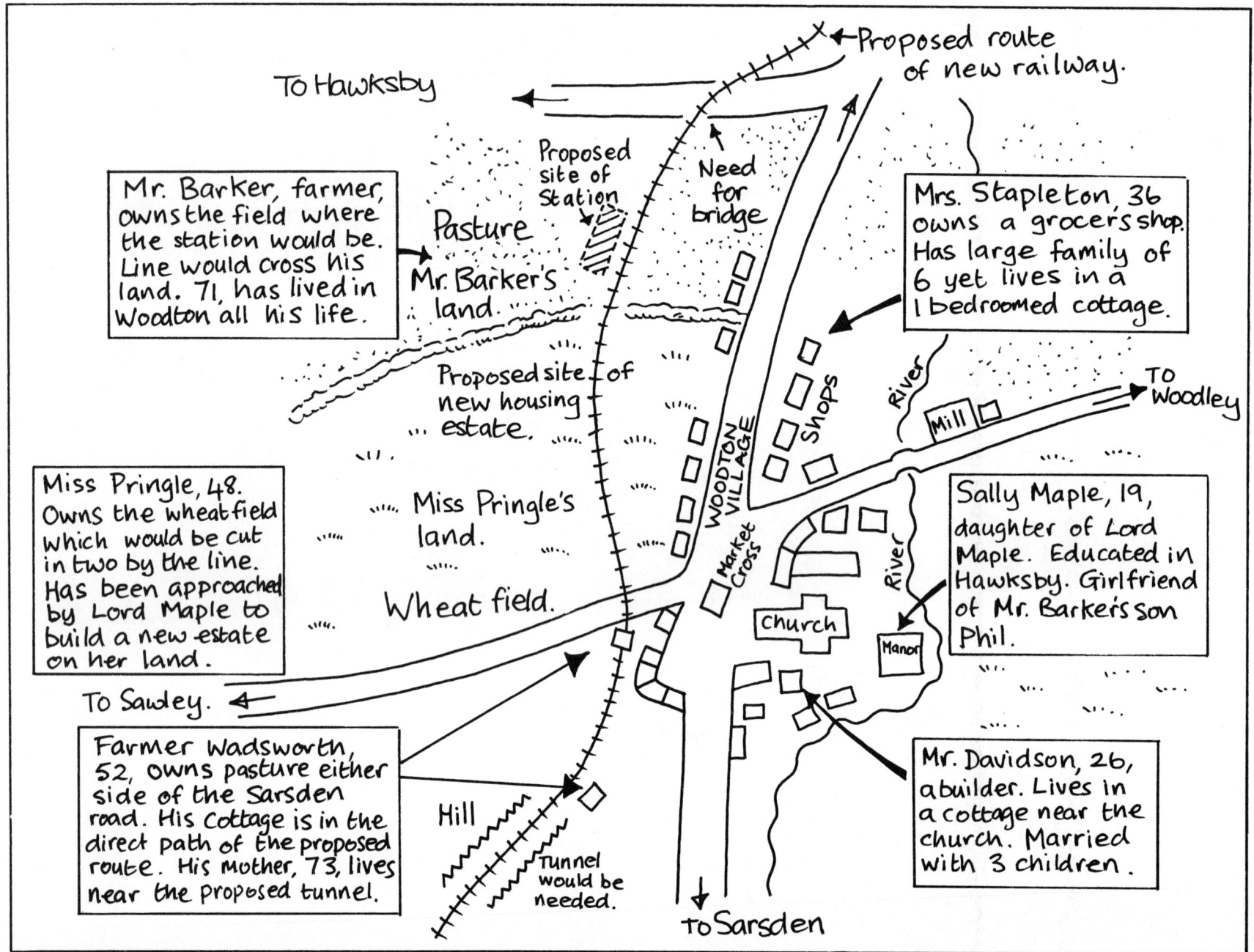

To Hawksby

Proposed route of new railway.

Proposed site of Station

Need for bridge

Mr. Barker, farmer, owns the field where the station would be. Line would cross his land. 71, has lived in Woodton all his life.

Pasture

Mr. Barker's land.

Mrs. Stapleton, 36 owns a grocer's shop. Has large family of 6 yet lives in a 1 bedroomed cottage.

River

To Woodley

Proposed site of new housing estate.

Shops

Mill

Miss Pringle, 48. Owns the wheatfield which would be cut in two by the line. Has been approached by Lord Maple to build a new estate on her land.

Miss Pringle's land.

WOODTON VILLAGE

River

Sally Maple, 19, daughter of Lord Maple. Educated in Hawksby. Girlfriend of Mr. Barker's son Phil.

Wheat field.

Market Cross

Church

Manor

To Sawley.

Farmer Wadsworth, 52, owns pasture either side of the Sarsden road. His cottage is in the direct path of the proposed route. His mother, 73, lives near the proposed tunnel.

Hill

Tunnel would be needed.

To Sarsden

Mr. Davidson, 26, a builder. Lives in a cottage near the church. Married with 3 children.

Inset (top left, Scotland):

The only British canals to receive any financial assistance from the Government were the CALEDONIAN and CRINAN.

CALEDONIAN CANAL constructed to save long and dangerous journey round North coast.

CRINAN CANAL avoids sailing round KINTYRE

FORTH & CLYDE

Inset (bottom left, Liverpool/Manchester):

To collieries at Worsley

MANCHESTER

R. Mersey

The Canal from Worsley Collieries to Manchester was completed in 1761. The price of coal in the town was halved.

Liverpool and Manchester opened 1830

Grand Trunk Trent and Mersey Canal

LIVERPOOL

MERSEY

Portions of rivers Mersey and Irwell deepened 1720-1740

Duke of Bridgewater's Canal 1767

Manchester Ship Canal 1894

Main map labels:

Before the INDUSTRIAL REVOLUTION there were few roads across the Pennine moors. The great industrial development after 1760 necessitated the construction of THREE canals despite the engineering difficulties involved.

NEWCASTLE
TYNE

HULL

YORK
OUSE
LEEDS
AIRE
DON
SHEFFIELD
LEEDS & LIVERPOOL CANAL
WIGAN
MANCHESTER
LIVERPOOL
TRENT
NOTTINGHAM
MERSEY
BURTON
TRENT AND MERSEY
STOKE
GRAND TRUNK OR
LEICESTER
GRAND UNION
COVENTRY
BIRMINGHAM
OXFORD CANAL
(COAL FROM MIDLANDS)
WORCESTER
SEVERN
SHREWSBURY
CHEESE/SALT/LIME
GRAND JUNCTION CANAL
SUGAR/TEA
THAMES
HERTFORD
LEA
NEWBURY
KENNET
BRISTOL
AVON
Coalfield

LEEDS & LIVERPOOL CANAL constructed 1769-1810 improved facilities for conveying raw materials and manufactures to port of Liverpool and manufacturing towns of West Riding and South Lancashire. Goods to and from the Baltic no longer required the long coastwise journey between Liverpool and Hull.

GRAND TRUNK CANAL constructed 1766-1777 carried Cheshire salt, Staffordshire pottery and Burton beer: the port of Liverpool greatly benefited.

Canals were built along most of the main River valleys of Wales. Those in the colliery valleys of South Wales were very prosperous before the advent of the railway, one of the great difficulties was the large number of locks necessary in this mountainous country.

Many canals were built in Southern England but they were little used after the coming of the railway.

N.B. Only the important canals have been shown.

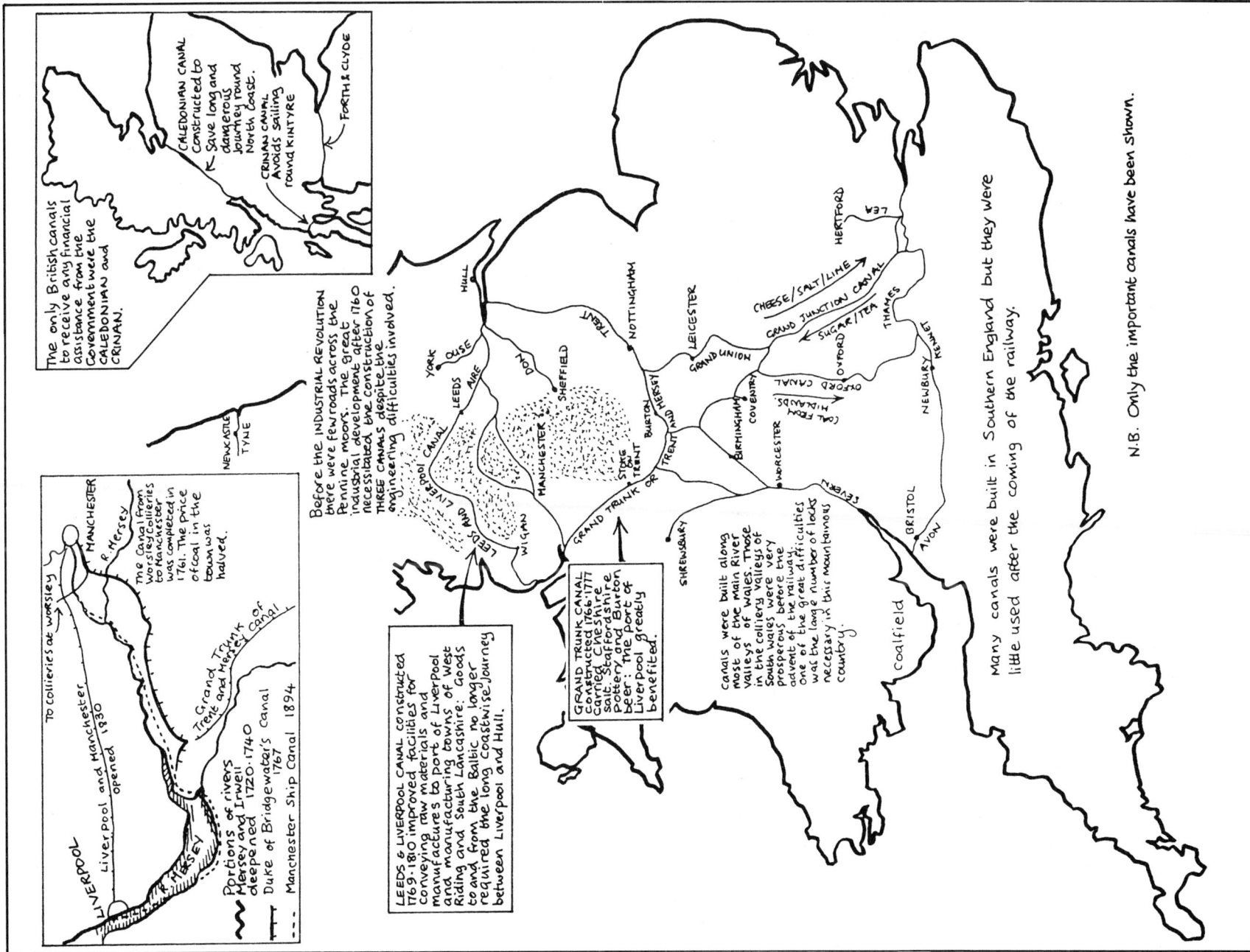

Story of a marriage, see page 45

CERTIFIED COPY OF AN ENTRY OF MARRIAGE   GIVEN AT THE GENERAL REGISTER OFFICE, LONDON

Application Number ___7436291___

18**39**. Marriage solemnised _Westfield_ in the _Church_ of _Stanton_ in the County of _Oxford_

No.	When Married.	Name and Surname.	Age.	Condition.	Rank or Profession.	Residence at the Time of Marriage.	Father's Name and Surname.	Rank or Profession of Father.
6	April	Jack Brown	26	Batchelor	Labourer	Stanton	Jack Brown	Farmer
		Anne Jowatt	23	Spinster	Servant		Albert Jowatt	Labourer

Married in the _Church of Stanton_ according to the Rites and Ceremonies of the _Church of England_ by me, _John Andrew Smith_

This marriage was solemnised between us, { Jack Brown his mark X Anne Jowatt her mark X } in the Presence of us, { William Brown his mark X Mary Brown her mark X }

CERTIFIED to be a true copy of an entry in the certified copy of a register of Marriages in the Registration District of _Westfield_
Given at the GENERAL REGISTER OFFICE, LONDON, under the seal of the said Office, the __14th__ day of _December_ 19 **89**

This page may be photocopied for use in the classroom and should not be declared in any return in respect of any photocopying licence.

7 June 1935   # The Birmingham Mail   One penny

BIRMINGHAM WIDOW FINED

Unemployed Woman's Theft from Shop

A widow who told the court that she and her daughter had only 25s. to 30s. a week to live on, and the rent was 22s. 6d. a week, was fined 40s. or 21 days at Birmingham Police Court today by Alderman W. E. Lovesey and Alderman Grist. She pleaded guilty to the theft of two frocks from the wholesale warehouse of Bell and Nicolson, Ltd. She was Florence Bullivant (aged 42), who gave an address in Rann Street, but was stated to be living in rooms at Kenilworth Place, Francis Road, Edgbaston.

Alderman Lovesey observed that the time had come when all such cases would be dealt with by imprisonment. Fines did not seem to have any deterrent effect.

BOY ACCIDENTALLY DROWNED

"Accidental death" was the verdict at the inquest in Birmingham today on a six-year-old boy, Reginald Dennis Wood, son of George Wood, a metal cleaner, 84, Frances Road, King's Norton. The boy was drowned in the canal near Lifford Lane where, while walking with another boy, he tried to recover a piece of wood from the water and fell in.

FATALITY ON TESTING TRACK

The Birmingham coroner today adjourned till June 13 the inquest on Arnold George Knox (aged 23), a motor cycle tester of 52, Priory Road, Hall Green, whose death followed an accident on the testing track at the B.S.A. works, Sparkbrook, where he was employed.

WARRANT FOR A VICAR

Non-appearance in Bankruptcy Court

The Rev. Dr. Samuel Shannon, Vicar of St. Luke's, Leicester, failed to appear at Leicester Bankruptcy Court today, and the Registrar (Mr. C. Squire) issued a warrant for his arrest.

The Registrar stated, however, that in order that Dr. Shannon's parishioners should not be deprived of his ministry the warrant would lie in the office for ten days.

Mr Squire said that the vicar had written asking that the proceedings be cancelled, as he did not wish to become bankrupt.

"Dr. Shannon," the Registrar remarked, "must be taught that his cloth will not protect him from the jurisdiction of the court."

Mr. Evan Barlow, the Official Receiver, stated that when the papers were served on Dr. Shannon at the vicarage he threw them on the ground and, touching them with his stick, said: "I don't want them".

Mr. Barlow added that in a notice posted on a door in St. Luke's, Dr. Shannon asked the public to help him with a House of Lords appeal, and stated that he owed no-one any money.

HOLIDAY AIR CRASH

Englishman's Fatal Injury in Germany

Mr. C. J. Highfield, licensee of the Old Crown Hotel, Slough, who crashed at Baden Baden in a private aeroplane yesterday, has died of his injuries. He was accompanied by two friends and they also were badly injured.

Mrs. Highfield left for Germany yesterday in a specially chartered aeroplane from Croydon Aerodrome to be with her husband.

Mr. Highfield was stated to have both ankles, his jawbone, and the toes of both feet broken. He and his friends had been making a holiday air tour of Germany, and were on their way home.

Published by courtesy of the *Birmingham Post and Mail*

Street furniture, see page 66

Sun-dials

Link snuffer

Horse-drawn coach notice

Mason's mark

Merchant's mark

Hitching ring

Mounting block

Grating

Plaque

BMA
SIR. CHARLES
HASTINGS
1794 TO 1866

Memorial

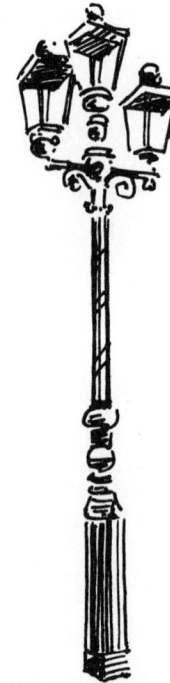

Victorian lamp-post

Statue

Pargetting patterns, see page 70

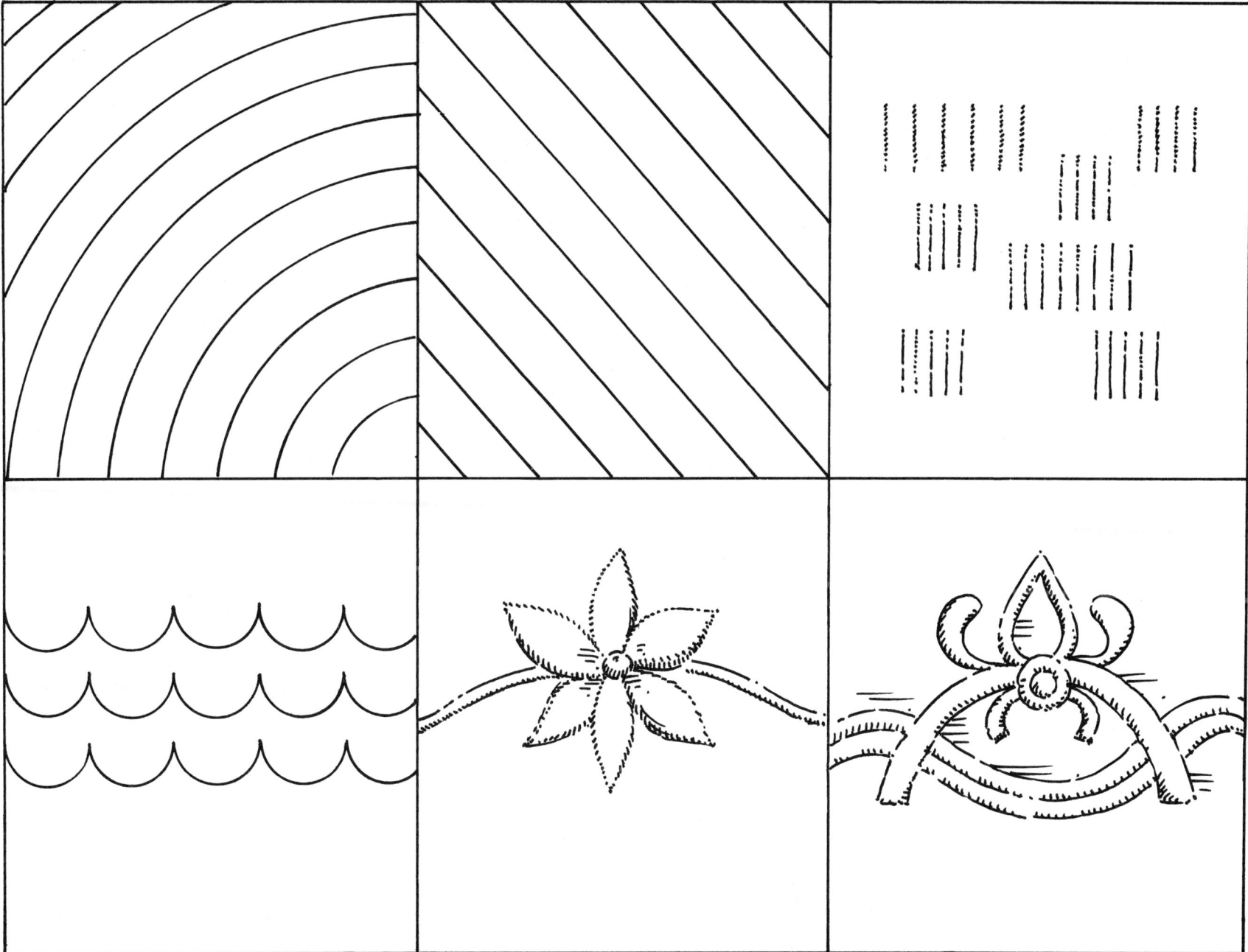

Stamp sorting, see page 77

1968

1978

1966

1974

1940

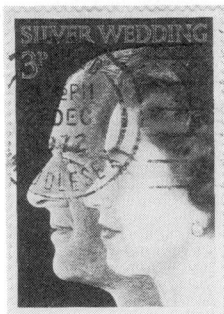

1972

1967

1973

1964

1966

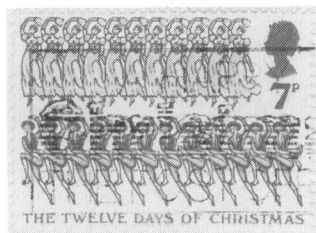

1977

1966

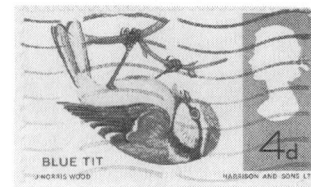

1966

1964

1978

1965

1991

Stamp sorting, see page 77

Morse code, see page 78

A	.—	H	....	O	———	V ...—
B	—...	I	..	P	.——.	W .——
C	—.—.	J	.———	Q	——.—	X —..—
D	—..	K	—.—	R	.—.	Y —.——
E	.	L	.—..	S	...	Z ——..
F	..—.	M	——	T	—	
G	——.	N	—.	U	..—	

Patchwork, see page 81

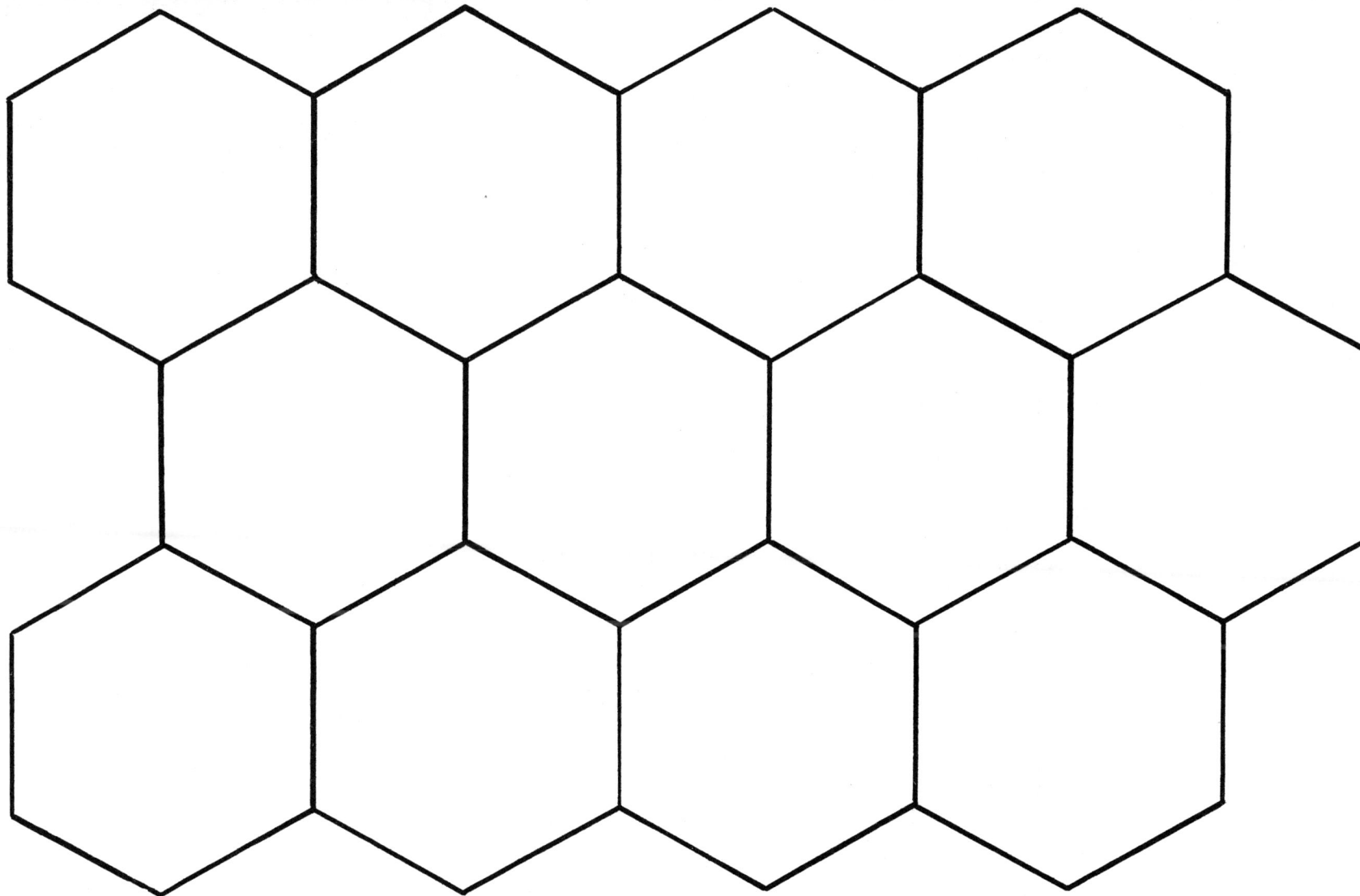

Use these hexagon shapes to record your patterns.

Quilt pattern, see page 82

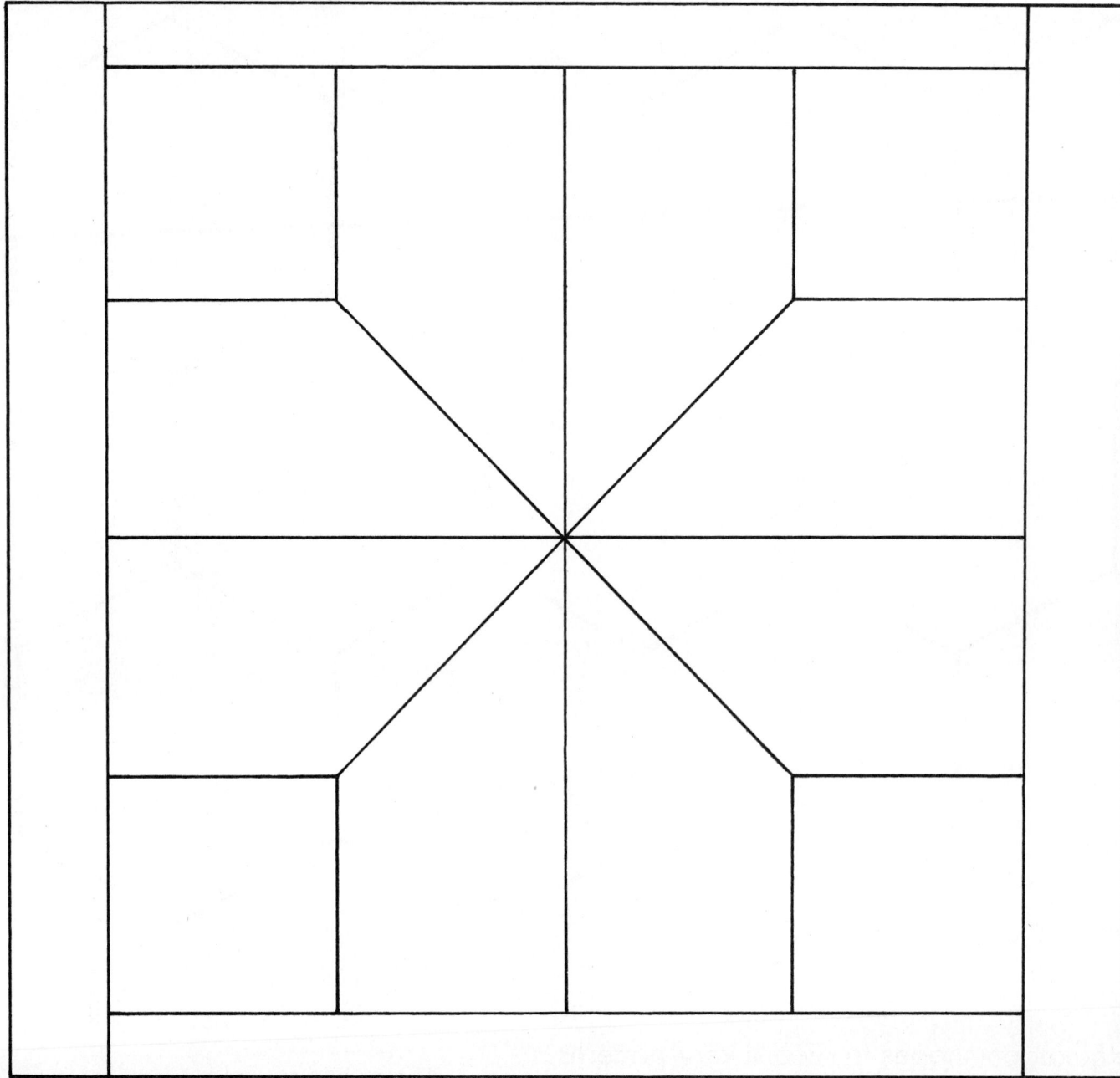

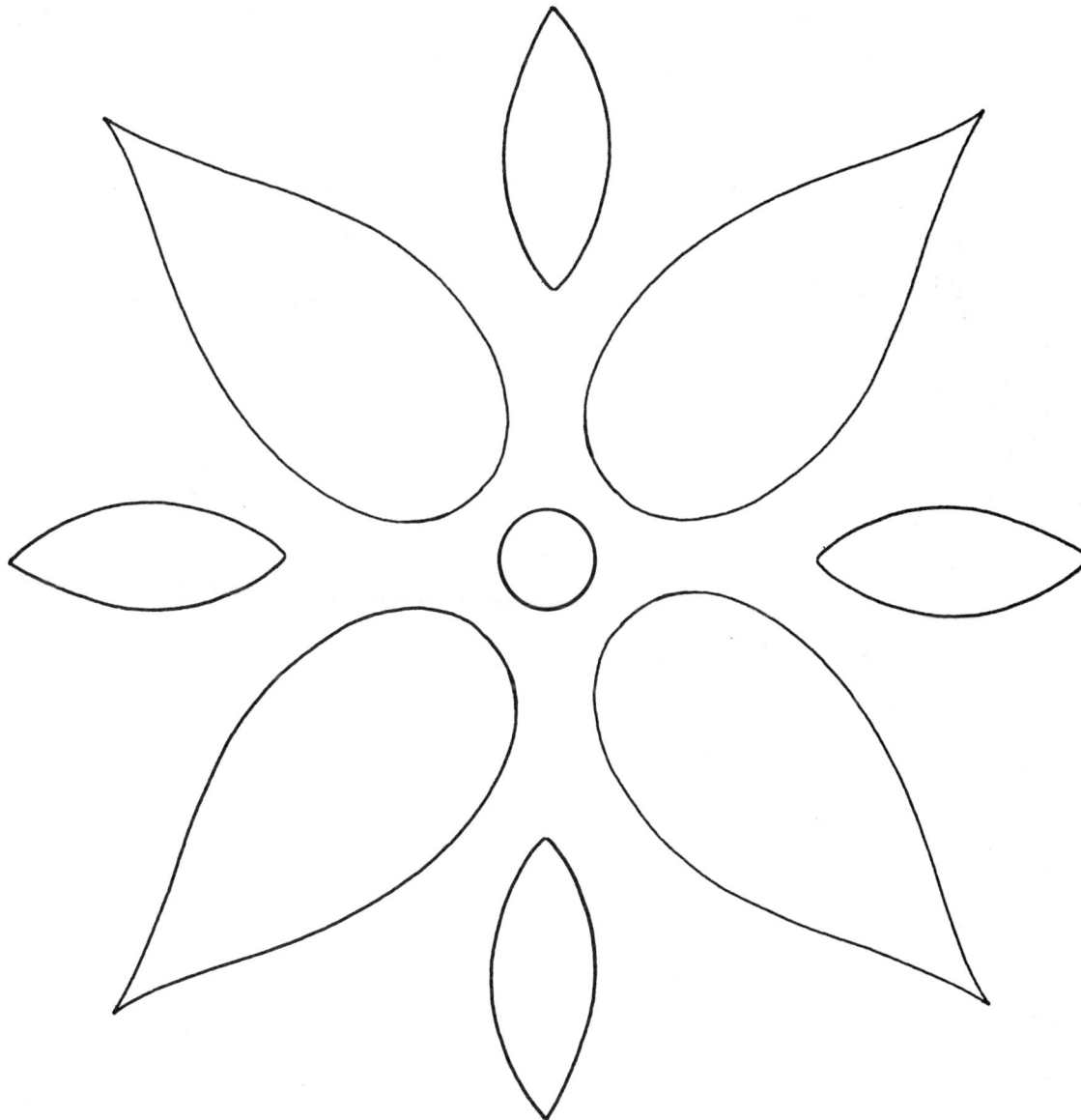

Below is an extract describing some of the methods employed by the putters – young people who dragged the coal from the coal face to the pit-bottom.

The labour in which children and young persons are employed in this district, next in severity to the sore slavery of coal-bearing, is coal-putting, in which we find the sexes more equally distributed. Putters drag or push the carts containing coal from the coal-wall to the pit-bottom; weight varying from three to ten hundred weight.

The following represents the mode of putting backwards with the face to the tub.

The boxes or carriages employed in putting are of two sorts, the hutchie and the slype; the hutchie being an oblong square-sided box with four wheels, which usually runs on a rail; and the slype is a wood-framed box, curved and shod with iron at the bottom, holding from 2 to 5cwt. of coal, adapted to the seams through which it is dragged. The lad or lass is harnessed over the shoulders and back with a strong leathern girth, which behind is furnished with an iron hook, which attaches itself to a chain fastened to the coal-cart or slype, and is thus dragged along. The dresses of these girls are made of coarse hempen stuff, (sacking), fitting close to the figure, the coverings to their heads are of the same material; little or no flannel is used, and their clothing, being of an absorbent nature, frequently gets completely saturated shortly after descending the pit, especially where the roofs are soft.

Where the seams are narrow and the roofs low, children and young persons of both sexes drag on all fours, like horses.

Period houses, see page 94

Medieval Cruck
cottage

Wattle and daub
15th & 16th century

Timber frame
15th & 16th century

Tudor

Elizabethan

Renaissance style
(Elizabethan)

Jacobean

Late Stuart
mid 17th century

Georgian
18th century

Adam style
18th century

Regency

Early Victorian

Late Victorian

Resources

Books for teachers

Adams, G. (1989) *Museums and Galleries*, Hutchinson.
Blyth, J. (1989) *History Teaching in the Primary School: A practical approach for teachers of 5–11 year olds*, Open University Press.
Blyth, J. (1988) *History 5–9* Hodder and Stoughton.
Blyth, J. et al (1990) *Place and Time with Children Age 5–9*, Routledge.
Blyth, J. and Low-Beer, A. (1990) *Teaching History to Young Children*, Historical Association
Cooper, H. (1992) *The Teaching of History*, David Fulton.
Cox, K. and Hughes, P. (1990) *Early Years History: an approach through story*, Liverpool Institute of Higher Education
Cues Community Division and Geffrye Museum (1988) *Black Contribution to History*, Geffrye Museum Publication.
Dickinson, A. K. and Lee, P. J. (eds) (1978, out of print) *History Teaching and Historical Understanding*, Heinemann.
Durbin, G., Morris, S. and Wilkinson, S. (1991) *A Teacher's Guide to Learning from Objects*, English Heritage.
Fairclough, J. and Redsell, P. (1985) *Living History – Reconstructing the Past with Young Children*, English Heritage.
Fairley, J. (1983, out of print) *History Teaching Through Museums*, Longmans.
Harrison, P. and Harrison, S. (1991–3) *History and Geography for Key Stages 1 & 2*, Simon & Schuster.
Hill, C. and Morris, J. (1991) *Practical Guides: History*, Scholastic Publications.
Key Stage 1: Teachers' Source Book 1–3 (series), Simon & Schuster.
Key Stage 2: History 1–2 Teachers' Book and Resource Pack (series), Simon & Schuster.
Little, V. and John, T. (1991) *Historical Fiction in the Classroom*, Historical Association.
Morris, S. (1989) *A Teacher's Guide to Using Portraits*, English Heritage.
Perks, R. (1992) *Oral History: Talking about the past*, Historical Association.
Pluckrose, H. (1991) *Children Learning History*, Simon & Schuster.
Steel, D. and Taylor, L. (1973, out of print) *Family History in Schools*, Phillimore.
Thompson, P. (1988) *Voice of the Past*, Oxford University Press.
West, J. (1986, out of print) *Timeline History Pack*, Nelson.
Wilson, V. and Woodhouse, J. (1992) *History Through Drama*, Historical Association.
Wright, M. (1992) *The Really Practical Guide to Primary History*, Stanley Thornes.

Places to visit

Angus Folk Museum
Kirkwynd
Glamis
Angus
DD8 1RT

Avoncroft Museum of Buildings
Stoke Heath
Bromsgrove
Hereford and Worcester
B60 4JR

Bethnal Green Museum of Childhood
Cambridge Heath Road
London
E2 9PA

Bexley Museum
Hall Place
Bourne Road
Bexley
Kent
DA5 1PQ

The Black Country Museum Trust Ltd.
Tipton Road
Dudley
West Midlands
DY1 4SQ

The Birmingham Museum of Science
and Industry
Newhall Street
Birmingham
West Midlands
B3 1RZ

The British Museum
Great Russell Street
London
WC1B 3DG

The Bromsgrove Museum
26 Birmingham Road
Bromsgrove
Hereford and Worcester
B61 0DD

The Canal Museum
Stoke Bruerne
Towcester
Northamptonshire
NN12 7SE

Chatterly Whitfield Mining Museum
Tunstall
Stoke on Trent
Staffordshire
ST6 8UN

Clarke Hall Educational Museum
Aberford Road
Wakefield
Yorkshire
WF1 4AL

Cogges Manor Farm Museum
Church Lane
Witney
Oxfordshire
OX8 6LA

The Council for British Archaeology
112 Kennington Road
London
SE11 6RE

Cutty Sark Clipper Ship
King William Walk
Greenwich
London
SE10 9HT

English Heritage
Education Service
Keysign House
429 Oxford Street
W1R 2HD

Exeter Maritime Museum
Haven Road
The Quay
Exeter
Devon
EX2 4AN

Fitzwilliam Museum
Trumpington Street
Cambridge
CB2 1RB

Forty Hall Museum
Forty Hill
Enfield
Middlesex
EN2 9HA

Gallery of English Costume
Platt Hall
Platt Fields
Rusholme
Manchester
M14 5LL

Geffrye Museum
Kingsland Road
Shoreditch
London
E2 8EA

Greenwich Borough Museum
232 Plumstead High Street
London
SE18 1JL

Group for Education in Museums
389 Great Western Road
Aberdeen
AB1 6NY

Gwent Rural Life Museum
The Malt Barn
New Market Street
Usk
Gwent
NP5 1AU

Hampton Court Palace
East Molesey
Surrey
KT8 9AU

Hatfield House
Hatfield Park
Hertfordshire
AL9 5NF

Historical Association
59a Kennington Park Road
London
S11 4JH

Imperial War Museum
Duxford Airfield
Duxford
Cambridge   CB2 4QR

Ironbridge Gorge Museum Trust
The Wharfage
Ironbridge
Shropshire
TF8 7AW

Jorvik Viking Centre
Coppergate
York
YO1 1NT

Kidwelly Industrial Museum
Kidwelly
Dyfed
SA17 4LW

Llechwedd Slate Caverns
Blaenau Ffestiniog
Gwynedd
LL41 3NB

The Lock Museum
54 New Road
Willenhall
West Midlands
WV13 2DA

London Toy and Model Museum
21-23 Craven Hill
London
W2 3EN

London Transport Museum
Covent Garden
The Piazza
London
WC2E 7BB

Lullingstone Roman Villa
Lullingstone Lane
Eynsford
Dartford
Kent
DA4 0JA

Maesllyn Woollen Mill Museum
Llandysul
Dyfed
SA44 5LD

McLean Museum and Art Gallery
9 Union Street
Greenock
Renfrewshire
PA16 8JX

Merseyside Maritime Museum
Pier Head
Liverpool
Merseyside
L3 1DN

Midland Motor Museum
Stanmore Hall
Stourbridge Road
Bridgnorth
Shropshire
WV15 6DT

Museum of Childhood
42 High Street
Royal Mile
Edinburgh
EH1 1TG

Museum of Childhood
1 Castle Street
Beaumaris
Gwynedd
LL58 8AP

Museum of the History of Education
University of Leeds
Springfield Mount
Leeds
LS2 9JT

Museum of London
London Wall
London
EC2Y 5HN

Museum of Transport
Kelvin Hall
1 Bunhouse Road
Glasgow
G3 8DP

Museum of the Welsh Woollen Industry
Dre-fach Felindre
Llandysul
Dyfed
SA44 5UP

The National Gallery
Trafalgar Square
London
WC2N 5DN

The National Maritime Museum
Park Row
Greenwich
London
SE10 9NF

The National Motor Museum
Montagu Ventures Ltd.
The John Montagu Building
Beaulieu
Hampshire
SO42 7ZN

The National Portrait Gallery
2 St Martin's Place
London
WC2H 0HE

The National Postal Museum
King Edward Building
King Edward Street
London
EC1A 1LP

The National Railway Museum
Leeman Road
York
YO2 4XJ

The National Trust
36 Queen Anne's Gate
London
SW1H 9A5

Penhow Castle
Penhow
Nr Newport
Gwent
NP6 3AD

Royal Research Ship 'Discovery'
Discovery Point
Discovery Quay
Dundee

Science Museum
Exhibition Road
South Kensington
London
SW7 2DD

The Scottish Agricultural Museum
Ingliston
Newbridge
Midlothian EH28 8NB

The Scottish Fisheries Museum Trust Ltd.
St Ayles
Harbourhead
Anstruther
Fife
KY10 3AB

The Scottish National Portrait Gallery
1 Queen Street
Edinburgh
EH2 1JD

Scottish Tartans Museum
Davidson House
Drummond Street
Comrie
Perthshire
PH6 2DW

Spitalfields Heritage Centre
19 Princelet Street
London
E1 6QE

Tredegar House and Park
Newport
Gwent
NP1 9YW

Weald and Downland Open Air Museum
Singleton
Near Chichester
West Sussex
PO18 0EU

The Welsh Folk Museum
St Fagans
Cardiff
South Glamorgan
CF5 6XB